NIGHT OF THE U-BOATS

Also by these authors and available from NEL:

P.Q. 17 - CONVOY TO HELL
TRAWLERS GO TO WAR

Night of the U-Boats

Paul Lund &
Harry Ludlam

NEW ENGLISH LIBRARY
TIMES MIRROR

First published in Great Britain by W. Foulsham & Co. Ltd., 1973

*

FIRST NEL PAPERBACK EDITION MAY 1974

*

NEL Books are published by
New English Library Limited from Barnard's Inn, Holborn, London E.C.1.
Made and printed in Great Britain by Hunt Barnard Printing Ltd., Aylesbury, Bucks.

45001833 4

SC7 was one of many convoys to sail the North Atlantic. This book is written to the memory of them all, and the men who sailed and escorted them.

Of the events that have taken place during the last few hours of this 'Black Friday' I will write again if we are spared to get through this next day and night. Suffice to say at present that I was never so glad and thankful that during these months I have been back at sea I have each day said my prayers as I have been in the habit of at home. I am sure that during the last twenty-four hours only something higher than any good fortune has enabled us to be still sailing on this Saturday morning. For which fact I shall always return thanks.

— From the shipboard diary
of Radio Officer Kenneth
Howell, ss. *Corinthic*;
dawn, October 19th, 1940.

CONTENTS

INTRODUCTION

The Darkest Days

OCTOBER, 1940. In this fourteenth month of the war with Germany, Britain stood alone with her back to the wall. After a winter of 'phoney war' the year had seen disaster after disaster. The withdrawal from Norway. The fall of Denmark, Holland, and Belgium. The evacuation from Dunkirk and the capitulation of France, followed by Mussolini's entry into the war on the side of Hitler. Day by day, the rolling tide of Nazism had spread over the newspaper maps of Europe like some great black evil blot.

Young men had gone fresh to Norway and France and returned disillusioned, though not beaten, veterans. The carefree notes of the popular song 'We're Going To Hang Out The Washing On The Siegfried Line' had gone sour.

Now, invasion of England by the Germans seemed inevitable.

The first enemy onslaught in the skies had been beaten off gloriously by the RAF in the Battle of Britain, but now hordes of German bombers were coming nightly, as many as a thousand planes at a time. In London, where on some nights bombs fell every few minutes, the sky raged red from the glare of burning buildings. Stabbing fingers of criss-crossing searchlights sought the deep droning high flying bombers; there was the thump-thump-thump of anti-aircraft guns and the whistle of bombs; explosions, alarms and cries, and shrapnel hissing down in the streets.

At this time of crisis people anxiously scanned the newspapers and listened for the news on the BBC, sturdy reliable voice in a tumbling world. The communiques, coming between such reassuring programmes as 'Hi Gang', 'Thanking Yew!' and Sandy Macpherson at the organ, were grim. They were days of 'Music While You Work' and nights of misery, death and stubborn heroism. By the end of September, the month in which the great bombing Blitz began, seventeen thousand men, women and children had been killed or seriously injured in the savage air-raids. In bleak October the casualties continued to rise.

Above it all, despite the constant hammering of enemy Channel ports by the RAF, hung the dark cloud of imminent invasion. Churchill frankly admitted to the nation that Germany had ships and barges ready to transport an army of half a million men to the beaches of Britain - if they could make the crossing. 'We are waiting,' he said pugnaciously. 'So are the fishes.'

Also waiting were a thousand British fighting ships of all descriptions, some three hundred of which were always at sea on anti-invasion patrol. Many of these ships had been withdrawn from duties in the Atlantic and the Western Approaches for the emergency, with the consequence that convoys crossing to Britain from Canada were desperately short of escorts for the ocean voyage. And the warships that sailed out to meet the convoys and bring them safely home were also severely depleted in numbers.

Losses of merchant ships had risen alarmingly as the rampaging U-boats grew in numbers and daring. Since June, 1940, the losses had multiplied, until in September, U-boats sank fifty-nine ships of 295,335 tons, most of these off the northern coast of Ireland, well named the Bloody Foreland.

It was now the blackest period of the sea war, the zenith of four months' slaughter which the U-boat commanders were to look back on as 'the happy time.'

At first only fast convoys had sailed homeward across the Atlantic from Halifax, Nova Scotia. These 'HX' convoys were made up of ships capable of maintaining a steady eight or nine knots. But to increase the flow of supplies across the ocean lifeline and to make use of slower ships, a second type of convoy was begun. These were the 'SC' convoys, which sailed from Sydney, Cape Breton Island, Nova Scotia. The plan was to sail these convoys of old, slow cargo vessels during the good summer weather, taking sixteen days to complete the passage at a laborious six or seven knots. But the urgency of the situation demanded that they should continue to sail throughout the winter. And so ships that had never before risked the hard and turbulent waters of the North Atlantic in winter had the special light loading line drawn at the base of the loading marks on their sides; the mark for WNA - 'Winter North Atlantic'. And into the teeth of winter they sailed.

SC7, the seventh of the slow convoys, sailed from Sydney, Cape Breton, at twelve noon on October 5, 1940. It was a convoy of thirty-five ancient ships carrying mundane, if vital, cargoes of timber, grain, steel, scrap and iron ore. It was nothing special. It might have lost one ship or a few, then won through to home waters and been quickly forgotten, just another convoy among hundreds.

But it did not happen that way. SC7 sailed into history as the victim of one of the biggest and most painful surprises sprung by the Germans in the war at sea.

This is the story of convoy SC7, and the men who were there.

I

The Admiral's Daughter

Within hours of the long awaited telegram arriving in Cleveland, Ohio, two attractive young mothers were in the air, their gay little red and blue aeroplane firmly on course for Halifax, Nova Scotia, a thousand miles away. They had only one parachute between them, and for Fynvola James it was only her second time in a plane, but Mary King was an experienced pilot and this was all set to be one of the happiest flights she had ever made.

It was October 2, 1940. The telegram had told Mrs James the glad news that her father, a retired Admiral now back in service as a Commodore of convoys, would be able to see her at Halifax before leaving for Britain with his next convoy. Mrs James had sailed out to Cleveland with her three young children in the grim, uncertain days following Dunkirk. Now, with her father and her husband, a naval commander in the Admiralty, both far away in the war, this brief chance to see her father was not to be missed. Mrs King, who owned the plane, had seen to that.

The Stinson light aeroplane flew due east at its one hundred-plus miles an hour, following the shore of Lake Erie, then on to Schenectady to land and fill up with thirty gallons of fuel to take them on to Portland, Maine, by nightfall. On they flew, over tree-covered hills in the full glory of autumn scarlets, yellows and oranges, and bright blue lakes that reflected the white clouds above. After an overnight stop at Portland, the Stinson took off at dawn for Bangor, the last airport inside the United States. There it landed on a bumpy runway and filled up with fuel to the brim for the non-stop flight to Halifax, for with Canada at war the two women had been warned not to land anywhere else than their permitted destination.

There were no maps of Canada available in wartime, nor were there any radioed weather reports or flight instructions; the plane's radio now remained stubbornly silent to their every call. After the busy, friendly airwaves of neutral America, it was very disconcerting. It also made the flight much more difficult. All Mary King had to navigate by was an ancient road map of very small scale, and as they flew on across wild, wooded country they hugged the one and only road for most of the time, it being their only hope of making a forced landing should the plane's single engine fail them.

But it did not, and they successfully reached the port of Saint John, New Brunswick. Here again, though, there was still no reply from the radio, and after circling round fruitlessly they headed east across the Bay of Fundy to Nova Scotia. It was the shortest and quickest route, instead of going north and swinging round to Halifax overland, and they were in a hurry, for it was only a matter of hours before the Commodore was due to leave to join his convoy. But crossing the bay meant flying over twenty miles of open sea in their small one-engined landplane. They held their breaths, murmured a prayer, crossed their fingers . . . and reached the far shore. From then on it was an easier journey, flying overland, and at noon they sighted Halifax harbour, but still with the radio eerily silent in spite of their repeated calls.

They were now at the end of their thousand-mile trip, looking down on the port where the ships gathered for the big convoys to Britain - they counted no fewer than sixty vessels waiting at anchor. But where was the airport? As the radio gave no help they looked again at the old road map. It indicated an airport on the north side of the harbour, and sure enough, on searching around they sighted it - a fine big one, it appeared. They circled it once, then Mary King brought the Stinson gently down to land.

Unbelieving eyes watched the little red plane taxi to a halt in the middle of the airfield, where great camouflaged bombers stood ready with their deadly loads. For this was the airfield of Eastern Air Command, Royal Canadian Air Force. Scarcely had the plane's wheels stopped before a plain clothes detective jumped in shut the doors and windows and started to question the two women, while a Mountie stood guard outside. Crowds of curious airmen gathered round to see the plane and catch a glimpse of its two most unlikely occupants.

The plane had been silently tracked through the skies from the moment it had come wandering over the border - it had come very, very close to being shot down. Who were they? asked the detective, and where were their papers? The two spirited young women obediently handed over their documents. Everything had been planned for the flight and the necessary papers obtained from Washington as soon as Mrs James had first heard by letter that her father would be coming to Halifax. Everything, they said, was in order.

But it was not. Some vital landing permits were missing, and Mrs King realized, too late, that Washington had neglected to send them to her.

Now the questions came thick and fast They were going to meet father? Who was father? Vice-Admiral Lachlan Donald Ian MacKinnon, CB, CVO. Where was he? Oh . . . er . . . he must be waiting at the civil airport. After a flurry of telephone calls the little plane was taken away and locked up, and the two 'suspects' driven from the airport under police escort.

So Mrs James was eventually reunited with her father under circumstances which neither they nor the Royal Canadian Air Force were ever likely to forget. Fortunately the admiral's departure had been postponed by one day, so that he was able to accompany the two women as they went from one office to the next, swearing in triplicate who they were and answering a battery of official questions, while the authorities checked with Washington and delighted newspaper reporters jostled for the story of the saucy flight. What a lark and a laugh and a gift for the front page to relieve the gloomy news from the old country.

Even after the admiral had gone it still took his daughter and her friend another twenty-four hours to get things sorted out to every official's satisfaction. Then, with smiles all round, the Stinson aeroplane, considerately polished until it shone, was released from its locked hanger, filled up with fuel, and Fynvola James and Mary King climbed back into it for their thousand mile journey back to Cleveland, armed with navigation papers kindly provided. The airmen stood around and waved, and waved . . . but the plane did not move. Mary King had carefully put the main switch in a safe place and now couldn't find it. There followed a minute or two of deep embarrassment while everyone took a turn at searching the plane, then the switch was found - put tidily where it should have been. The Stinson took off, circled and vanished into the sky, and the Royal Canadian Air Force shook its head in wonderment and went back to war.

Admiral MacKinnon, meanwhile, having seen the funny side of the affair in spite of all the fuss and bother, had left by train for Sydney, Cape Breton, to take up his next convoy. He was last seen by his daughter walking off with a light suitcase containing all his personal belongings. In itself an unusual sight, for it was so at odds with the important naval life which he had led before Hitler's war began.

Lachlan MacKinnon, the son of a parson, had joined the Royal Navy as a thirteen-year-old cadet in the days of Queen Victoria. Now, a grey-haired fifty-seven, he looked back on an eventful career. The first World War had seen him as gunnery officer of HMS *Indomitable* at the Battle of Jutland, service which gained him special promotion, and he went on to become the first commander of the proud new battle cruiser HMS *Hood*. MacKinnon was always a man of the big ships, and always zealously on top of his job, whether as captain of a cruiser in the China Seas or, in later years, as Rear-Admiral commanding the 2nd Battle Squadron, Home Fleet. His multitude of honours included the award of the CVO for organizing the King George V Jubilee review of the Fleet in 1935, though a lesser known but especially pleasing honour was the result of his service as an instructor to the Turkish Navy when a young lieutenant. The Turks dubbed him 'Mac Kinnon Bey.'

MacKinnon was not a tall man, but he bore himself very erect and was a stickler for deportment. He could not abide to see a man with his hands in his pockets. He was a disciplinarian, and liked to see things done just right. But he also had a zest for living coupled with a deep sense of humour. He enjoyed gay company, and as a senior officer in the big ships was able to indulge in, and organize, the social round. Although used to having officers and men jump to his every need and command, and quietly enjoying the fact, he was extremely popular with both. He was Navy through and through, but possessed of a vivid personality that was not bound by the gold braid.

Had war broken out earlier, as threatened at the time of the Munich crisis in 1938, when he commanded the 2nd Battle Squadron, Admiral Lachlan MacKinnon would have jumped straight into an important active service command. Instead, the immediate threat of hostilities receded, and the following January, after forty-two years in the navy, he retired. When, only months later, war came after all, he was quickly back to volunteer his services. But his situation had changed. He was offered a post as Commodore of Convoys.

There could hardly have been a greater contrast with his past career. The Commodore of a convoy sailed in one of the merchant ships and was responsible for keeping the merchantmen in formation, passing them signals for altering course, zig-zagging and other evasive manoeuvres, and generally keeping some order among the flock, working in liaison with the senior escorting warship. The Commodore's 'flagship' could vary from a substantial cargo-liner to a dirty old tramp, and his staff was never more than a handful of naval signalmen. A far, far cry from other days. But Lachlan MacKinnon, like many another retired senior naval officer or merchant officer of the Royal Naval Reserve who took on the onerous job of Commodore, put into it all he knew. Though the standard of signalling among the merchant ships, to say nothing of their station-keeping, was enough to try the patience of a saint, he had adapted himself to the job with a keeness and level temper that brought good results.

Only once in several convoys had he been known to air a mild complaint; about the master of his 'flagship' whose billious delight it had been to stuff himself with steak and cabbage for breakfast every day.

Long before Commodore MacKinnon caught the train for Sydney, the ships that were to form convoy SC7 had been loading their cargoes in readiness for the homeward passage.

Some went to ports of the United States for their loads. To New Orleans, in the south, for grain and aluminium ore; and to Baltimore, in the north, for strip-steel, pig-iron and scrap. Some of these vessels then continued on to New York to top up their cargoes with more loads of food, pitprops, railway lines and scrap. It was hardly a wildly exciting cargo, a load of junk iron and steel dumped aboard by a giant magnetic grab, but it was precious enough. As some United States Army ordnance officers had worked out very precisely, from every ton of American scrap iron, Britiain could manufacture either one 75-millimetre field gun, twelve machine-guns, one 16-inch battleship piercing shell, or nine 500 pound bombs.

All they had to do, of course, was to get those precious tons across the U-boat infested Atlantic.

But the great majority of ships destined for SC7 went to load up at Canadian ports, some of these so small and outlandish that ships' captains had never heard of them and had to call in at other ports first to ask the way. However, soon all these vessels were busy taking aboard their cargoes at various points in an area of activity stretching high up the eastern coast of Canada.

For some ships the loading port was the familiar one of Saint John, chief port of New Brunswick, on the Bay of Fundy. Here they took on timber, copper ore, steel, grain and trucks. Others went up to Campbellton, the hunting, fishing and lumber centre, to take on a full cargo of timber - rough-sawn planks of varying lengths.

Other ships journeyed still farther north to Gaspe, on the Gulf of St. Lawrence. Here the local men and girls came down to watch as great bundles of pitprops were swung aboard. The winches worked in pairs, one doing the lifting and the other the swinging of the cargo. Once the holds were filled, additional logs were stacked on top of the steel decks of the steamers, like thousands of giant matchsticks.

Some vessels had to make the journey into the St. Lawrence River itself, up past Anticosti Island, where great schools of whales played, blowing their steaming breath a stone's throw from the ships, leaping spectacularly and then plunging deep from gaping gazes. Two busy river loading ports were Quebec, city of a million lights on both sides of the river, and Rimouski, the pilot station of the St. Lawrence, where the pitprops could be seen rushing down the hillside in long troughs of flumes, into which local streams were diverted high up the slopes. After their spectacular wet glissades, sawmills in the valley cut the long logs into short lengths with far-ringing noises and puffs of white steam.

Farther up the St. Lawrence at Three Rivers, ships loading grain anchored alongside a gigantic grain elevator with many cylindrical storage buildings more than two hundred feet high. A discharge tunnel ran down to the quayside and from it came four large pipes which swung out over the holds of the ship to be loaded. With a hiss a torrent of grain would start pouring in a dusty golden cascade into four holds at once, the dust soon settling over the ship like pale fawn snow.

At Three Rivers, too, ships came to load steel and timber. Two such vessels were the *Beatus* and the *Fiscus*, big steamships of nearly 5,000 gross tons. Both were built in the 1920s and hailed from Cardiff, where they were among the best kept ships in and out of that port, each a fine floating advertisement for her owners, the Tempus Shipping Company.

Captain Wilfred Brett took the *Beatus* into Three Rivers for a load of oblong steel ingots weighing five tons each. Once these were safely stored down in the lower holds *Beatus* took on a load of timber laid on top of the steel and also piled twelve feet high on deck. The cargo for *Fiscus*, on the other hand, was composed almost entirely of the steel ingots, together with a number of large crates containing aircraft repaired in Canada for return to the U.K. *Fiscus*'s master, Captain Ebenezer Williams, looked on with sad eyes as the two ships were loading and observed with much feeling, 'I wish I had your cargo instead of mine . . .'

Captain Williams did not seem his usual self. At forty-eight, he was nine years older than Captain Brett of *Beatus* and had done his turn at sea during World War I. Never a talkative man at the best of times, he now seemed full of the gloomiest forebodings. He was due for leave on his return to the U.K., but seemed convinced that he would never see his home in Anglesey again. He confided these fears to other masters, too, and would not be consoled. In truth there was not much they could say. When it was common knowledge that a ship loaded with steel, like *Fiscus*, could sink like a stone when torpedoed, there was little one could reply to his firm presentiment of disaster, except to encourage him to have faith in God and the convoy.

Far to the north, round the eastern hump of Canada, on the coast of Labrador, other ships steamed in to collect their cargoes of timber. Two which found their way to the little-known port of Francis Harbour, at the mouth of the Alexis River, were the *Scoresby* and the *Clintonia*. Smaller ships these, and older, the *Clintonia* having braved the assaults of U-boats in the last war. Francis Harbour was not much of a place, there was hardly anything there but the church of St. Francis after which it was named. For *Scoresby* the load was 1,586 fathoms of pitprops slung and heaved up straight from the river; many had been spilled out by a ship which came to grief on rocks near the coast. The props had been rounded up into rafts secured by chains, and were brought alongside *Scoresby* and winched aboard in slings. The props were stowed below and on the decks, and over all the hatches including the cross-bunker hatch. This meant that one had to climb a makeshift ladder outside the crew quarters aft, the apprentices' quarters for'ard or the saloon entrance, and get to the top of the cargo before being able to see around the horizon. But although so well loaded *Scoresby*, and other timber-carrying ships like her, were not laden to danger point and all had to take in water ballast to counter top weight for seaworthiness for a normal sea journey.

Clintonia's load was pulpwood, also fished straight out of the water. The pulpwood floated at an anchorage in the sea near the beach, enclosed by big booms; it was towed out to the ship and winched into her holds.

And so it went on, the ships that were to join SC7 taking on their loads at a dozen different ports. Not only British ships but many of other nationalities, vessels which had either been taken over by the Ministry of War Transport after the collapse of their countries or which were still neutral but chose to sail in British convoy rather than cross the Atlantic alone. Neutrals were always offered this choice, and the majority wisely decided that there was more safety in numbers. Hitler had yet to make his stormy declaration that 'every ship with, or without convoy, which appears before our torpedo tubes is going to be torpedoed,' but for months the U-boats, in complete disregard of international law, had been doing exactly that, regularly sinking neutral as well as Allied merchant shipping round the coasts of Britain. Huge national flags painted on the sides of a neutral vessel never stayed the passage of a death dealing torpedo.

One of three Swedish ships destined for SC7, the small 1,500-ton *Gunborg*, was outside the enemy blockade when the Germans swarmed across Norway, and so like many vessels had been chartered by the British authorities. Her arrival now at St. John's, Newfoundland, to pick up a cargo of pulpwood was of fateful importance to one young Swedish seaman.

Sture Mattsson, just sixteen years old, was hardly yet recovered from the shock of having his ship go down beneath him on the voyage across to Canada. He had come out in convoy in a Swedish ship which was torpedoed and sank in two and a half minutes, taking down with her many of his shipmates. Young Mattsson was among the survivors picked up by a British ship called the *Empire Soldier* and brought to St. John's, where he had been for six weeks when the *Gunborg* called. He had lost all his possessions, but had been kitted out and told he could go home to Sweden by a Swedish ship sailing from New York to Petsamo, in Finland. This was fine offer, and yet the lad could not bring himself to accept it. It had a lot to do with something he had heard the master of the *Empire Soldier* say. The master, Captain H. A. Lego, was an old man in his seventies, drawing a well earned pension. One day Mattsson heard someone ask him why, at his time of life, he should still be at sea, to which Captain Lego quietly replied, 'If there is something I can do for old England, this I want to do before I die.'

It was a modest remark that made a profound impression on the young Swede, as did another incident involving the old captain. When *Empire Soldier* picked up Mattsson and the other survivors her crew threw a wooden-runged rope ladder over the side for them to climb up. Unfortunately the ladder struck the wife of the Swedish ship's engineer on the head and split it open. Calmly, Captain Lego set to and expertly sewed up the wound. It was a fine piece of work that earned the congratulations of doctors at St. John's.

So Sture Mattsson chewed it all over and went to the anchored *Gunborg*, which was bound for the Clyde, and found they needed an able-seaman. His friends all advised him to take passage home to Sweden, but he firmly did not heed them. He shouldered his seabag, collected his pet dog and stepped aboard the ship due to sail with SC7.

The previous SC convoy, SC6, had left Sydney, Cape Breton, on September 27. Soon after its departure the first of the motley ships of SC7 began to arrive.

Unlike in blacked-out Britain, Sydney wore its lights at night, and an intermittent heavy glare came from a point on shore near the steelworks, where white-hot slag was tipped at the water's edge. Some ships of the SC convoys took on their loads of steel at Sydney and went on to top up with timber elsewhere, then return. It was no hardship to leave Sydney for there was nothing prepossessing about the place for seamen to remember. Those who went ashore found a ramshackle main street of wooden houses where they waited for a bus into town. The town itself seemed very much a shanty affair, though there were also some substantial brick buildings. But anyway, who was here for the sights? The one appeal of Sydney was that it was the last stop on the way home.

On a warmish day at Sydney it was tempting to go over the side for a swim, though those who attempted it soon clambered out again fighting off an attack of the shivers. The water was always far colder than the sun made it look. In deep winter the harbour became covered with pack-ice and often froze over altogether, so firmly that the local inhabitants could drive their cars over the ice.

A swim would have been welcome after the business of coaling up. Ships bunkered at the coaling station of St. Pierre across the bay, where from great wooden erections trucks ran out to supply the shutes. Coaling-up shot coal all over the decks, while fine coal dust invaded all rooms and cabins and got up everyone's nose. It was a mercy if it rained. In the evening after the day's toil, crews might go ashore to a dancehall where strong men in lumber jackets swung girls around in the air in true lumber-camp style while the band played nothing but variations of the tune 'Blueberry Hill' all night.

As the ships earmarked for SC7 were entered in the official lists, so the structure of the convoy began to take shape. There would be about thirty-five ships in all, half of these British. The foreigners would include the three Swedes, six Norwegians, four Greeks, a French tanker, two Dutch ships and one Danish.

'Old wrecks and barnacled tramps' was the laconic description unofficially applied to the greater part of the convoy. It was not far from the truth. For what the convoy papers did not show was that half the ships of SC7 were old vessels dating back to World War I and some even to the turn of the century. The four venerable Greek ships, for instance, had sailed the oceans under a total of ten different names, the oldest vessel among them having carried her first cargoes way back in 1906. But the Norwegians had the oldest ship of all. She was the small and ancient steam tanker *Thoroy*, built as long ago as 1893! *Thoroy* was a credit to her British builders, Armstrong Mitchell of Newcastle, who had constructed her in those pioneer years of tanker building. Launched as the petroleum tanker *Snowflake*, she had become a veteran of the high seas long before the Boer War began, and had sailed for forty-seven years under four different names and nationalities. She excusably drew the admiration of other SC7 masters, mainly for the fact that she was still cheekily afloat.

Several of the other foreigners were also British-built and formerly British owned.

At least two ships in the convoy should have sailed with the previous SC convoy, but to their shame had missed it, while two others had been directed to one of the fast HX convoys from Halifax, but had to drop out when found woefully incapable of keeping up the required speed. They were then shuttled off to join 'the slow buggers' at Sydney. There were no illusions about the vessels sailing in the SC convoys, least of all among naval control; as one senior officer admitted, ships were sailed from Sydney that would never have been given a seaworthy ticket in peacetime.

Among the British ships of SC7 was one which had actually lain under water for some time. Several vessels had been resurrected from rusting graves pegged out for them during the great shipping depression of the 1930s. This was especially true of the tramp steamers, vessels which in normal times had no fixed routes but touted their way around the seas, available to any merchant who could provide a cargo, working from one port to the next, lifting cheap and handy bulk loads such as they were now carrying for war. The depression had laid up hundreds of tramps and other cargo vessels to idle away their days at desolate moorings until, in December 1939, the Ministry of War Transport began requisitioning them; when overnight, almost any vessel that could still ride the water became at once precious and vital to the country's needs.

Such a ship saved from a rusting eternity was the *Corinthic*, from Hull. She had been laid up for years in the River Fal in Cornwall, the tourists' river which, during the depression, had held as many as eighty unwanted ships, a never-ending line of silent, ghostly vessels inhabited only by nightwatchmen. *Conrinthic*, on her earlier voyage out of the United States, had arrived twelve days overdue, having spent many hours on many days quite motionless at sea, while her engineers sweated to repair various peculiar breakdowns. A hair-raising experience, knowing that at any moment she could be the target for a scavenging U-boat. Now here she was, reporting for SC7 laden with another eight thousand tons of scrap and steel, though this time with her crew feeling quite swanky, for the heavy junk cargo was topped by a somewhat more respectable load of railway lines, plus a pile of strip-steel for plating aeroplanes. *Corinthic*'s fiery little master was Captain George Nesbitt from Hull, who had reason enough for not being very fond of Germans. When World War I broke out he was in a British ship lying in a German port, and was promptly interned for the duration of that war. Captain Nesbitt was resolved that Hitler's war would not find him so easily removed from the fight.

Another British ship rescued from the scrapheap was the *Botusk*, from London. This strange, jungle-sounding name was not the one with which she had started out in life. In common with some other vessels her name had been changed to give her the prefix 'BOT', standing for Board of Trade. Meanwhile, the dubious honour of being the oldest British ship in the convoy was shared by two hard-worked vessels dating back to 1912. One was the *Creekirk*, now loaded with iron ore for Cardiff, and sailing under her third name since leaving the Glasgow shipyards so long ago. The other was the *Empire Brigade*, which after an eventful career had been sold to Italian owners, but was back in the fold after being taken in prize by the Royal Navy on Italy's entry into the war and given her third, resoundingly English, name.

Among all this odd assortment of ships, however, the strangest by far were three British vessels from the Great Lakes of North America. All the other ships of SC7, even the smallest and rustiest old tramp, pitied the Lakers - 'Too bloody slow to get out of their own way!'

The Lake boats - never 'ships' - were weird looking vessels with a high bridge-house set almost on the bow, and a funnel placed well aft, above the engines. With their long, flat midships in between, it was as if the people at each end of the vessel would never meet. Nor did they, except at mealtimes in the messrooms aft, for in the bow section lived the captain, his deck officers and crew, while back in the stern section lived the engineering staff and stewards. But it was all to a purpose in the Lakers' natural habitat; the curious forward bridge-house was to give the captain maximum visibility when negotiating the narrow channels connecting the Great Lakes.

Even if the Germans did not pounce on these 'sweet water' vessels the winter storms of the Atlantic must surely break their slender backs, thought the ocean seamen. But in fact all three boats, two of them less than 2,000 tons, had been built in Britain and sailed across the Atlantic to begin their life on the Lakes. Admittedly this ocean voyage had been made in the best of weather conditions, in high summer, and they had not tasted salt water since, nor ever been intended to. Yet now, after long years spent carrying cargoes round the island ports of the Great Lakes, here they were, facing the uncompromising Atlantic at the stormy time of year. And this with puny engines of around a hundred horse-power or less, compared with the 300-plus horse-power of the most elderly ocean freighter.

Masters and crews had been sent out from Britain to bring over the Lakers. It was to be a once-and-for-all crossing for the vessels, carrying timber cargo to help keep them afloat, for on reaching Britain they would be put to work round the coast mainly as coal-carriers. But whether they could make the journey was another matter. The unexpected antics of the first Lakers to attempt the passage, sailing in the calmer days of August with SC1, left the Commodore of that convoy totally bemused. 'I had five Lake boats,' he said, 'which appeared to yaw 60 degrees each side of their course, but later I discovered that this is their method of advance if they think they are closing ahead.' One of the five was so helpless she had to return to Sydney only hours after SC1 sailed, while another had to turn back the next day. The harassed

Commodore thought he would also have to write off the remaining three, but to his surprise they were still in sight next day and gradually took up their correct stations, though their steaming eccentricities continued throughout the voyage. Two other Lakers which set out with SC4 in September found it difficult to keep pace with the convoy even in a smooth sea, and in rough seas later could hardly move. Yet to everyone's astonishment and delight they still won through.

But it was now October, and how SC7's three Lakers would fare in this month's wild seas was anybody's guess.

This, then was the motley collection of ships which Commodore Lachlan MacKinnon was to lead across the Atlantic. These, and one other, the British steamer that was to be his 'flagship'. Her name was *Assyrian*.

As the Commodore took the train for Sydney, *Assyrian*'s captain was ploughing his ship there along the east coast of Nova Scotia. Neither of them knew of their forthcoming meeting, nor could they have had any idea of the arduous course on which Fate had, even now, launched them both.

2

A Ship Called Fritz

The *Assyrian* was actually a vessel from the other side. The Germans had built her at Hamburg in 1914 as the *Fritz*, but at the end of the Kaiser's war she was handed over to Britain as a reparations ship. When the Ellerman and Papayanni Lines acquired her they rechristened her *Assyrian*, and at their hands she changed much more than her name.

The Germans had built *Assyrian* as a diesel engined motorship, one of the first of her kind ever to put to sea. But on joining the Ellerman fleet she was very soon converted to a more conventional steamship. In the hard costing of a British cargo vessel, pared down to the smallest fractions of a penny, there was no room for new-fangled diesels. For one thing it was difficult to get spares for the engines, and for another, they needed to be operated by twelve engineers! So out came the Sulzer diesels, and in went the steam engines.

To save expense, it was decided to keep *Assyrian*'s original propeller shafting and propellers. This complicated matters as it limited the choice of suitable engines, but she was eventually fitted with two trawler-type steam reciprocating triple-expansion engines. Old-fashioned and slower they might be, but infinitely more reliable.

So *Assyrian* became a coal fired twin-screw steamship, though keeping at least one tangible reminder of her revolutionary origin.

Her mainmast was still fitted with the running gear which had enabled her former German crew to hoist a trawlerlike sail whenever her experimental diesels became troublesome.

For the next twenty years, from her new home port of Liverpool, *Assyrian* voyaged about the oceans of the world on different trades, striving to achieve a ten-knot average for at least one voyage but never quite managing it. In calm seas and light winds she might maintain nine knots steaming flat out, but in heavy weather her progress was likely to be no more than four or five knots.

On being requisitioned for war service she first worked in the Mediterranean, carrying general cargoes, until Italy came into the war. Then she was transferred to the Atlantic. As she had no such refinements as a refrigerator, only an ice-box, carrying perishable foods for lengthy periods made things difficult as far as the crew's feeding arrangements went, as the ice dwindled; but still, with all her limitations *Assyrian* was a well loved 'old tub.'

Early in August 1940 she loaded up at Liverpool with a cargo for the West Indies. She carried a gun now. It was fitted in the Barry Roads, an old four-pounder of 1914-18 vintage, set up on the after deck. Some of her crew went ashore for brief instruction on how to use it. The first time they fired the gun it shook everything up both above and below her wooden decks, and broke the bottom of the ice-box. Ah well, maybe it would cause bigger discomfort to the Germans. All hands eventually had some rudimentary training on it so that they could double as members of the gun-crew in an emergency.

Although she was a Liverpool based ship and so had many men from Cheshire and North Wales in her crew of thirty-nine, *Assyrian* also had men from Bristol, Hull and Devon, and some Irishmen.

Her master was Irish. Captain Reginald Kearon, a youthful thirty-five years old, came from a large seafaring family in Arklow. Stocky and well built, with black wavy hair and a healthily ruddy clean-shaven face, he was both a crisp professional mariner and a very likeable personality. Reg Kearon was not stand-offish, nor did he pull rank, and was greatly respected by all hands, with whom he enjoyed mixing freely as 'one of the lads.' His chief officer was Irish, too. John King came from Rush, in County Dublin. He was touching sixty and had served the shipping line for many years. But although to the younger elements in the ship's company he seemed a ripe old age, he lacked nothing in vigour and enthusiasm, and like his captain was popular with everyone. The other two deck officers, the second and third mates, were also well experienced men in their thirties and forties, while at the other end of the age scale the youngest crewman aboard was a cadet of sixteen.

It was to Captain Kearon's credit that he kept a happy ship in which almost every member of the crew got along well together. They all knew their job, although one or two among them were men who had been forced by the great shipping slump to quit the sea and find a job ashore . . . until war called them back. Like Robert Stracy, the ship's quiet-spoken radio officer. After being laid off during the slump which rendered one in every four British seamen unemployed, Stracy took a shore post, but remained in the Merchant Navy Officers' War Reserve, and so was hurriedly recalled for service at the outbreak of war. How ironically the pendulum had swung back for previously unwanted men and ships.

Assyrian's fateful passage to SC7 began when she left Liverpool in August. Five days out she lost her convoy and had to steam on alone south to Barbados, which she reached without incident. Her next call was at Georgetown, British Guiana, and here occurred a warmly sentimental interlude which, in the light of later events, was to become a poignant memory. Chief Officer John King had not seen his sister for some twenty years. She was a nun in a convent far out in the wilds of Brazil. The ship's agent, asked to pull a few strings for a faithful employee, had arranged that King should at last meet his sister, and from Georgetown he was flown several hours away to a midway point where she also had been flown to meet him. The chief officer was a very happy man when he returned to the ship two days later.

From Georgetown *Assyrian* steamed north through the Caribbean to New Orleans, there to load up for her return voyage across the Atlantic. In the light of the grave news from home, with hundreds dying nightly under the rain of enemy bombs and Britain facing an invasion by the might of the German armies it seemed a strange situation for them to be in, sailing through the sunny Caribbean playing deck quoits to while away the hours, Captain Kearon joining in with everyone, cook, firemen and all. To some, in fact, it seemed altogether wrong to be idling their time away in this manner when the old country was in such desperate straits and urgently in need of supplies. But *Assyrian* was forging on to do her bit in the best way she could.

After loading up with grain and other cargo at New Orleans

she made ready for the long voyage home. She was ordered to join a convoy going north from Bermuda to New York, there to top up her cargo, but in spite of the willing work of her twin screws she was quite unable to keep up with the convoy's fast speed of eight or nine knots and had to drop out and plod on to New York alone. Tumbling weather made this long journey an eventful one in which so much crockery was smashed that they were left with barely enough cups to go round. As a final disappointment she arrived at New York too late to catch another convoy sailing to Halifax, Nova Scotia, on the next stage of the journey home.

However, she made it to Halifax, and her arrival there brought particular joy to three French naval men. They were billeted in the *Champlain*, a French ship which had lain for a long time in the Bedford Basin, her crew undecided which side to be on after the fall of France. The three men had finally opted to throw in their lot with the Free French, and were accepted for passage to the U.K. aboard the first available ship. So Lieutenant Gabriele Andre Sauvaget of Bordeaux, and ratings Oliver Paupon and Marcel le Meur, an exuberant trio, happily joined the ship for the last leg of her voyage to join SC7. This was a journey some 230 miles north-east along the coast of Nova Scotia to Sydney.

She only just made it, arriving the day before the convoy was due to sail. But this was one convoy she would not - could not - lose, for to everyone's surprise they learned on arrival that they were to lead it. The old *Assyrian*, Commodore ship! Never in her twenty-six years had she known such an honour.

Down below, bespectacled William Venables looked over the engines on which he had lavished so much care during seven contented years as her Second Engineer.

Assyrian, at only 2,962 tons, was one of the smallest British ships in the convoy, besides being one of the oldest. But she could do it. Of course she could!

Commodore Lachlan MacKinnon boarded *Assyrian* late that evening, together with his staff of five naval petty officers and ratings: a yeoman of signals, two telegraphists and two signalmen. He was to share the captain's cabin, while his staff were found accommodation in the ship's four passenger cabins, where the Frenchmen, too, were berthed.

Chief Steward James Daley went ashore by naval launch to order the essential provisions needed to make good the ship's depleted stores. Plus a crate of crockery, for there was hardly enough left for the use of the ship's company, never mind the extra nine people now aboard. He was promised that the stores would be alongside by 10 a.m. the following morning, two hours before sailing time.

Just before midnight the big dark shape of the last of the British ships destined for the convoy nosed its way into Sydney harbour. She was the 5,000-ton *Somersby*, a West Hartlepool vessel carrying a cargo of grain.

Next day was Saturday, October 5, 1940. Dawn broke clear and bright over the groups of anchored ships and brought a warm morning sun. But with everyone due to move out on the stroke of noon there was little time to enjoy the weather. Breakfasts were cut short as launches picked up the merchant masters, together with an accompanying officer, and took them ashore for the official convoy conference.

It was not a very long conference. The masters were given the by now usual pep talk about keeping good station according to their allotted numbers in the convoy, which would take the general formation of six columns of five or six ships each. They were urged to act smartly on the Commodore's signalled instructions, and warned against lagging behind and becoming a 'straggler', with the probable dire consequences of collecting a torpedo from a prowling U-boat.

As the Navy strove to ram home its advice, the masters digested it all impassively in that deceptively casual manner which had caused an earlier Commodore to complain testily 'little notice was taken of points made by the officers speaking . . .' But there was another side to it. The SC briefings were by no means as well organized as the conferences at Halifax for the HX sailings, and it was still sorrowfully remembered how one SC Commodore had missed the conference altogether through being given the wrong orders.

The masters of SC7 learned that they were to have just one naval escort across the Atlantic, a little sloop smaller than the smallest tramp steamer among them. There would also be an armed yacht and an 'aerial escort' - a seaplane - for the first two days, but these would then turn back and the convoy would be on its way with only the sloop for protection until they reached the Western Approaches. No amount of pep-talking could make the one small warship seem any bigger, especially when considered against the limited, and in some cases ludicrous, armament of the merchant ships. Perhaps a dozen among them had an old four-inch or four-pounder mounted aft, two or three of these vessels having the added advantage of a Naval Reservist gunner to lead the merchant gun-crew. But other ships had only a machine-gun, or perhaps two, mounted on the bridge, while yet others had merely the odd rifle; like the British *Carsbreck*, whose sole defensive weapon was a rifle in charge of the chief officer. The more fortunate *Beatus*, which boasted on old four-inch on the poop, had also possessed two rifles . . . until these were taken away for anti-invasion use.

So SC7 would have to sail on for ten days until it reached the point of rendezvous where warships of the Western Approaches would come out to meet it and escort it in. With Hitler's big new ocean-going U-boats already reported to be ranging farther and farther west across the Atlantic, this seemed to be cutting it rather fine. But that's how it was.

A more optimistic note was struck when Commodore MacKinnon, drawing calmly on his pipe, was introduced as one who had never lost a ship in convoy - and who had no intention of blotting that record. The masters liked what they saw, a fit, precise and clear-thinking man, obviously well on top of his job. Even if he was a retired admiral.

And that was that. 'Best wishes for a safe passage, gentlemen . . .'

After the conference most of the masters had a drink and a chat before returning to their ships. Still full of gloom was Captain Ebenezer Williams of the steel laden *Fiscus*. He had heard nothing in conference to alter his conviction that this was to be his last voyage, that doom was staring him in the face. Could it be the Welshman's aptitude for second sight that had given him this persistent, nagging premonition of disaster? It was going to need great effort for him to hide his feelings from his crew.

Meanwhile aboard *Assyrian* Chief Steward Daley was a very worried man. Ten o'clock had come and gone, and there was still no sign of the promised stores. At 11 a.m., with the captain and Commodore now returned to the ship, he was called to the lower bridge. Where in heaven were the stores? asked Commodore MacKinnon. Daley told him of the assurance he had been given, but still the minutes ticked by and nothing arrived. At 12 noon the naval escort sloop slipped out of harbour and *Assyrian* was due to start leading the ships of the convoy. Daley was again summoned to the bridge. This time Commodore MacKinnon was pacing to and fro in exasperation. He was very displeased.

'Mr Daley, can we proceed without the extra supplies?'

Daley quickly ran his mind's eye over the ship's reduced stores, now required to feed an extra nine mouths. Yes, he said, they could just about get through if they used, in rotation, fresh, canned and salted meats, for luckily the ship had stored to capacity on canned meats at New Orleans. But bread was the big problem. The stock of flour would never last the journey. However, if they used part-bread and biscuits . . .

Ships around *Assyrian* had now begun to move off. A naval launch hove into sight and the Commodore took up a loudhailer and cracked an order to its officer in charge. 'Take an urgent message ashore,' said the Commodore grimly, 'that if this ship's stores are not alongside in fifteen minutes, someone's head will roll!' The launch shot off at speed.

To the consternation of the chief steward, *Assyrian* then started to get under way, the Commodore determined to make up for precious minutes lost and sail the ship to schedule. But after an anxious interval there came a gladdening shout from one of the crew - 'Chief, the stores have come.'

In response to the Commodore's fierce warning a hurried flotilla of motorboats chugged alongside the slowly moving ship and Daley and his staff quickly gathered aboard in welcoming arms sides of meat, bags of potatoes and flour, and a precious crate of crockery, managing to complete the loading just in time before *Assyrian* increased speed and steamed importantly out of harbour to head the convoy.

The good weather continued throughout the afternoon as the thirty-five ships ponderously took up their positions in the convoy formation, *Assyrian* at the head of the centre column and the escort sloop out in front, together with the armed yacht. And then, in the early evening, they were off. Unlike an earlier SC convoy, which had taken no less than twenty-nine frustrating hours to form up.

Meanwhile, back in Sydney harbour a latecomer for the convoy had arrived in the shape of the little Norwegian tramp *Sneland I* Her passage to Sydney had been a laborious one. After loading aluminium ore at New Orleans she had gone north to the Hampton Roads, Virginia, to get concrete protection for her wheelhouse. She was delayed there for a long time and when about to leave was so heavily encrusted with barnacles that she was unable to keep up with a convoy. So she steamed on alone to Halifax, where shore workers armed with long scrapers got to work and the ship was made to list with the aid of her ballast tanks so that some of the offending barnacles could be removed. Then on she ploughed to Sydney to join SC7.

As *Sneland 1* dropped anchor her master and chief officer went hurriedly ashore to the convoy office for instructions. Sorry, they were told, the office was short of convoy documents, but they could get a set from a naval launch in the harbour. Captain Laegland and his chief scoured the water for the launch but could not find it. They decided the best thing they could do was to carry on and try to catch up with the convoy - and just hang on to it.

So *Sneland 1* steamed out determinedly after SC7 and, like some tardy Disney cartoon character, managed to catch up with the dark ranks of the convoy during the night. She crept in on the starboard wing as the last ship of that column, and steamed on in comfortable station for all the world as if that had been her rightful position all along. She had no knowledge of the convoy and no papers, and would not be able to understand a single signal from the Commodore, whoever that might be. But she had caught her convoy!

3

The Steaming Herd

Sunday, October 6, and already SC7 had suffered its first casualty. It was a fine morning on this second day at sea, and in the excellent visibility ships gradually beame aware that one vessel was missing. She was the *Winona*, the oldest and biggest of the three Lakers, and therefore the most conspicuous. What had happened to her?

Aboard *Assyrian*, Commodore MacKinnon put a cross beside the name of *Winona* on his official convoy list. The Laker had turned back in the early hours of darkness of the previous night. Despite the efforts of her chief engineer and his staff, her dynamo had failed to operate, and much to his disappointment Captain John Stevenson of Newcastle had had to turn his ship and head back to Sydney for repairs.

So now there were two. Eyes went to the other Lakers, doggedly struggling along in their erratic fashion.

In a clement sea the convoy steamed steadily along at its planned speed of seven knots, sometimes in good order and sometimes in rather haphazard fashion after a change of course had been ordered by the Commodore, for already he was busy making signals and reflectively watching their effect. The seaplane droned through a clear sky overhead, and close at hand was the armed yacht, HMCS *Elk*, a converted mercantile vessel known in more tranquil days as the *Arcadia*. Out ahead, the escort sloop HMS

Scarborough led the smokily steaming herd, which now covered a sizeable piece of ocean. The length of each column of ships was some three miles, and the six columns sailing abreast presented a broad front three or four miles across.

It was a workmanlike formation, and yet the scene did not at all resemble an illustration from a textbook of war. Far from hiding their identities in drab anonymity, most of the ships, British and foreign alike, sported the colours of their respective shipping lines on their funnels. At the start of their war service the British ships had been painted an anonymous grey with buff superstructure, in accordance with Ministry of War Transport regulations, but on next painting ship they had promptly put their peacetime colours back on the funnels, and many had reverted to their more familiar black hulls. Now it seemed to add that extra touch of defiance.

HMS *Scarborough* herself was hardly a textbook warship. She had been launched in 1930 as a naval survey vessel, and had spent practically all her life pre-war in the China Seas. She still had a large charthouse built out over the quarter-deck as a continuation of the foc'sle deck, so that although the after gun mounting remained, there was no after gun. Her only big gun, mounted for'ard, was an old low angle four-inch of Japanese make which she had picked up off the jetty at Hong Kong. Stamped with the date 1920, it was, in plain language, a 'bloody awful old thing', yet it worked and had been put to good use on more than one occasion.

Scarborough just topped a thousand tons, rather more than half the size of the smallest freighter in the convoy. She was a good seaboat, though with a bit of a list to starboard and a tendency to buck and roll alarmingly in heavy seas. At such times a rope was stretched across the wheelhouse and the helmsman put his arms over the rope to steady himself and keep an even course. It was painful on the arms, but effective. The sloop's top heaviness was partly due to another legacy of her peacetime occupation, an extra large motorboat used for surveying, which she still carried on big davits on the port side. The cumbersome boat was a great nuisance, and as offensive to her good lines as the unsightly charthouse.

She had wooden decks, which a former commanding officer had demanded should be kept scrubbed and burnished bright. As at that time she had no deck hydrants, no means of pumping up water for scrubbing the decks, her crew had to lower heavy wooden buckets over the side and haul them up filled with sea water, a long and arduous process which was agony on the muscles of the scrubbers, none of whom would forget the weight of those buckets as long as they lived. War or no war, they were kept hard at it holystoning the decks until one day the tell-tale shine from the sloop's decks was reported by an aircraft, and to everyone's immense relief the practice was ordered to be stopped forthwith.

Since being recalled for war *Scarborough* had managed to scrounge two stripped Lewis guns, which were mounted each side of the bridge - a token defence, at least, against aircraft. Her only other artillery was a saluting gun, a ceremonial piece which fired at a fixed angle from one side of the ship only.

She had also kept the sensitive hydrophones used for surveying, not for her the newer asdic equipment for detecting the underwater enemy, but she did carry a good quota of depth-charges. And she had seen one major change. Gone, along with the burnished decks, was the commanding officer who had believed in the little sloop observing big ship 'bull', with the blowing of bugles and all the rest. Her commander now was a tall, athletic Dartmouth trained man who, as the lower deck soon concluded to their satisfaction, 'really knew his stuff.' As almost all *Scarborough*'s crew were naval regulars, this was no mean accolade.

Commander Norman Vincent Dickinson, at forty, had already fought one war. He entered the Royal Navy as a cadet in 1915, and during World War I served in the Grand Fleet as a midshipman in the battleship *Royal Sovereign*, gaining the DSC. After the war he specialized in physical training, putting cadets in the *Erebus* and at the Royal Naval College, Dartmouth, through their paces, also seaman boys at Shotley. Later, back at sea, he was squadron P.T. officer with the 1st Cruiser Squadron, and with destroyer flotillas in the Mediterranean, before becoming assistant superintendent of the Physical and Recreational Training School at Portsmouth.

Quick, firm and decisive in manner, Commander Dickinson was a popular commander not only because it was plain he knew how to handle a ship, but because he had a good sense of humour and was eminently more approachable than his predecessor. Immediately he took command there was a new and better spirit among *Scarborough*'s company.

Before taking up duties in the North Atlantic the sloop had acted as the lone escort for several convoys from the U.K. to Gibraltar. In the early months of the war this had been a comparatively trouble-free passage, with the U-boats concentrating nearer Britain's shores, but lately *Scarborough* had seen a good deal more action, and there had been a very hot time on the outward bound convoy she had helped to bring out of the Western Approaches before continuing independently to Sydney, several ships of the convoy falling victim to U-boats.

Scarborough's duty now was to get SC7 safely to the rendezvous in the Western Approaches where other escorts would meet them. There were no special plans of action arranged between the sloop and the Commodore ship other than the general tactics laid down for the convoy. Commander Dickinson and Commodore MacKinnon had met only briefly at the Sydney conference, and their sole communication now would be by means of flag and lamp, for wireless telegraphy - morse transmission - was to be avoided, and no ships yet were equipped with radio telephony.

Sunday continued fine, and late afternoon found the convoy sailing eastwards below Newfoundland in position 45 deg. 17 min. N, 55 deg. 43 min. W. Next day they could expect to sweep round the far eastern corner of Newfoundland and begin the slow, steady passage north and east across the North Atlantic in a great curve.

In the underground Operations Room in London the position of SC7 was plotted on the huge map covering the whole of one wall: another slow convoy had begun the long voyage home. In the meantime the previous convoy, SC6, was nearing the Western Approaches. From an Admiralty point of view the record of these slow convoys so far was satisfactory. Though a U-boat on weather-station had sunk one hapless ship of SC1 so easily that the German commander was able to cruise around and take striking photographs of his slowly sinking kill, the losses had on the whole been relatively few. Only SC3 had encountered any great U-boat activity, when at least two U-boats had been seen cruising on the surface at night, in and out of the convoy. But even then, only four vessels were lost, two of these on becoming stragglers, and official opinion was that these sinkings might never have occurred had not the convoy arrived at rendezvous a day too early. In fact, the losses of the SC convoys so far had been much more damaging on the naval side, two escort sloops having been sunk by U-boats. The main troubles of the convoys, as successively reported by their harassed Commodores, had been those of very bad station-keeping and signalling, particularly by the foreign merchantmen, painful weather conditions, persistent straggling and near collisions, especially when some SC convoys had cut dangerously across the course of outward-bound convoys. There was no reason to suppose that SC7 would experience anything more than these now common hazards.

As the convoy steamed quietly on during the second day, the lookouts took stock of their companion ships, some familiar, others not.

Smallest of all the merchant vessels was an old Norwegian tramp, the *Havorn*. She had been sailing the seas since 1902 under three different names, and was now bound for the Mersey stacked high with pitprops. She was little more than 1,500 tons, but in the eyes of her crew it was better to be small, they were far happier than the crew of the convoy's biggest vessel and its most tempting target. This was the French tanker *Languedoc*, a splendid new motorship of nearly 10,000 tons which had been taken under the British flag in tropical waters after the capitulation of France. Now *Languedoc* was on her way to the Clyde, having been ordered to join SC7 after missing a fast HX convoy. She was a most beautiful ship, very neat and clean and painted a smooth light grey. Cruising easily on the port wing of the convoy she stood out from the other vessels like a swan among geese, though her seeming pride did not extend to her cosmopolitan crew, headed by a British master. Being such a size meant being twice as vulnerable. In many another ship, too, they looked across at the big, sleek *Languedoc* and decided among themselves that if any ship was to be torpedoed, she would be the first to go.

The biggest British ship in the convoy, the 6,000-ton *Empire Miniver*, was not really British at all. In fact she was an American vessel of the 'three-island' type from Texas, and as old as the last war. Formerly the *West Cobalt*, she had been bought by Britain for war service - a sort of early lease-lend deal - and now carried a full load of steel and pig-iron on this, her second voyage to Britain under her new name, and with an all-British crew. Although like *Languedoc* she was oil-fired, and therefore a cut above the coal burners, *Empire Miniver*'s advantages beyond that were few. She had been used to carrying cotton, and her steel cargo made her very heavy and sluggish in her movements. Nor was her armament any more splendid than the rest. Her very old 4.7 in. gun, in charge of a Royal Marine Reservist gunlayer, had no protective shield, and its ammunition was in separate pieces consisting of shell, cordite bag and firing cartridge.

Less than half the ships in convoy had been 'degaussed.' That is, fitted with an electric cable run round the scuppers, which set up the ship's own magnetic field to counter magnetic mines. The 'degaussed' ships were easy to identify, a buff cross being painted on either side of the ship just under or just forward of the bridge structure. This was an official marking, and one criticized in blistering terms by the crews of the marked ships, for a better lining-up target for the crossed hairs of an enemy periscope could hardly be imagined.

Another uncomfortable target was provided by one of the Swedish ships, stubbornly intent on proclaiming her neutrality. The Swedish flag was painted large on her sides fore and aft, and the crosses were in luminous paint, which could be seen at night more than half a mile away. They were the cause of much anger aboard other ships, especially those nearest to her. Since when had any neutral flag deterred a U-boat?

There were many vessels which had already seen a fair bit of action.

The old *Trident*, a tramp from Newcastle upon Tyne, had even arrived at Cape Breton on her outward voyage carrying survivors whom she had rescued in mid-Atlantic. It happened that the *Trident* was steaming along one morning when there was a U-boat alarm from the bridge - they had sighted a lifeboat ahead with sails set. Captain Lancelot Balls thought the boat might be a decoy, but as it was dead ahead he kept on course with the gun-crew standing grimly by for action. However, it turned out that the lifeboat held seven survivors from the Norwegian ship *Karet*, which had been torpedoed at midnight. On their safe arrival at Sydney the grateful Norwegians presented *Trident* with a silver cocktail set, and the mates with fountain pens.

A brave ship was the old *Trident*, even if in bad weather she was always more under the Atlantic than on top of it, being constantly awash her earlier adventures she had escaped from Narvik with 10,000 tons of iron ore only hours before the Germans went in. A very cool master, Captain Balls. Once, when a periscope was sighted, he turned his ship full on to it so as to present a smaller target, clapped on all steam and prepared to ram the U-boat. Luckily for all, perhaps, the 'periscope' turned out to be nothing more than the mast of an empty waterlogged lifeboat from a sunken British liner.

Her crew loved the dirty old *Trident*, for she worked hard and always got through in her slow, ponderous way. They liked to joke that any U-boat commander who torpedoed her would get the sack for wasting a torpedo, for they reckoned she could fall to pieces at any time without any assistance from the Germans.

Empire Brigade, the ship snatched back from the Italians, had had a nerve-racking encounter with a U-boat on the way out, after losing her convoy. In heavy weather she suddenly came upon the U-boat on the surface and, each as surprised as the other, ship and submarine both fired one shell before the bad weather took over completely. The German's shell missed *Empire Brigade*, but the roaring gale that followed gave her a real hammering and shifted her centre castle back five inches; she had needed substantial repairs before she could join SC7. Her huge cargo now was 7,000 tons of copper ore, 3,000 tons of grain, great quantities of tinned foods, and eighteen Army lorries secured on the after deck.

At least one of the foreigners, too, had had an eventful outward journey from the U.K. This was the Dutch tramp *Soesterberg*. Her first fortunate escape had been when the east coast convoy with which she started out from Tyneside was attacked at night by enemy dive-bombers. Three ships immediately in company with *Soesterberg* were all struck by bombs, the convoy scattered and *Soesterberg* cracked on full steam to round the northern coast of Scotland and reach the waters of the Pentland Firth, south of the Orkneys. From here that same night she slipped out in the darkness and set course for Canada alone.

In the meantime the surviving ships of her convoy had re-formed and she was reported missing, believed lost. It was a tense lone voyage for *Soesterberg*. Three days out they thought their number was up when a plane swooped out of the clouds towards them, for no one aboard could tell one plane from another, friend or enemy, but resolutely they ran up the Dutch flag. The plane circled round, asking the name of the ship, and when they signalled this, it asked for a repeat. It then gave the recognition signal and disappeared in the direction of the English coast. The crew sighed with relief as the plane flew off . . . fortunately it was a British plane, which duly reported them to be still in the land of the living. And so *Soesterberg* had successfully made it to Canada to load up her vital cargo. Pitprops.

Sunday evening, and SC7 continued on course, sympathetic eyes again watching the two remaining Lakers steaming along in their peculiar manner, each looking like two metal islands with a stretch of white water in between. Crazy, just crazy, that vessels like these should have to make such a voyage.

Night came, a glorious night with the new moon shining as a new moon should, and the stars amazingly brilliant. Silent and dark, completely blacked out, the thirty-four ships progressed across the unusually calm and quiet ocean.

But the air waves were busy. Ships' radio officers picked up a message giving warning of a U-boat plotted at 51 deg. N, 27 deg.

W. *Twenty-seven degrees West!* With the convoy scheduled to meet its Western Approaches escorts much farther in, at twenty-one degrees West, this really was too close for comfort.

Monday, October 7. Dawn broke, bringing more remarkably settled weather. The sun shone brightly, the sea was very slight, and although the wind was not exactly warm, still it was far from cold.

An ideal day for putting the masters on their mettle. Commodore MacKinnon was active very early, exercising his charges in emergency alterations of course. As the radio officer in one steamer noted in his diary: 'Apparently this Commodore does the job properly!'

Aboard *Assyrian* it made them feel very important as the Commodore's signallers hoisted the bunting giving the orders, which were relayed throughout the convoy, ship to ship. This flag signalling would continue day by day, for complete radio silence had to be observed and the radio officers in the various ships kept a listening watch only. By night, the Commodore's signals were made by a system of red and green lights, a few selected ships being designated as light-repeating ships, so that the whole convoy did not hoist its lights and become lit up like the Blackpool illuminations. When each and every ship had digested the instructions, the executive signal actually to make the required manoeuvre came when the lights were switched off on the Commodore ship.

For the second day running the officers of *Sneland 1*, the barnacled latecomer, looked on in puzzlement at all the busy flag signalling without understanding any of it, not having any convoy papers; but this time the Commodore detected that something was wrong, and the ship ahead of *Sneland* was detailed to fall out of the column, drop back and take up position behind her, so as to be better placed to give assistance. But no sooner had this situation been sorted out than a ship appeared unexpectedly over the horizon ahead of the convoy, with the seeming intention of joining the flock.

The big British steamer *Shekatika*, only four years old but her steel decks already rusting, had set out from Halifax with a fast HX convoy, but found herself completely unable to stay the course. She was loaded with steel below, and pitprops piled high on her decks. In fact, so stacked with timber was she that the well-decks were full, and poles standing ten feet above the bulwarks prevented wholesale log cascades into the sea. Plank walks with wood handrails were nailed in place on top of the last of the mighty stack; by this means the crew walked from aft to duties amidships, and to the galley.

Shekatika had failed to keep up with the fast convoy mainly because of the poor quality Canadian coal in her bunkers. The firemen had done their best, coming up only to get great pickle jars of slightly salted drinking water at the galley pump. But no matter how hard they sweated and drank water to restore their body fluid, they could not keep the ship in station, especially at the end of each watch, when they 'ashed out' from the furnace great lumps of clinker six feet long. So Captain Robert Paterson had been ordered to turn back and join the slower convoy coming up in the rear. *Shekatika* was less than a day on her own before the ships of SC7 crept masts first round the curve of the world into her circle of sea, and at two o'clock in the afternoon she took up station as the last ship of the port column. Her armament? Just a single rifle used for anti-sabotage watch on the gangway when she was docked.

So, one ship gone, another gained. SC7 sailed on at seven knots. At 6 p.m., ships' clocks were advanced one hour. Clocks would be progressed the five hours from Eastern Time to Greenwich Time. At 9 p.m. the yacht HMCS *Elk* left the convoy for other duties, and the seaplane, too, was seen no more, The convoy was left alone with its single escort, the *Scarborough*, and would remain so for another ten days at least.

Just before midnight, course was altered for the night. And still the weather continued fine.

Tuesday, October 8. More settled weather, the morning sun shining brightly on the trim lines of ships. It took some believing . . . was this really the tempestuous Atlantic? There was a much bigger swell, however, causing ships to roll.

Commodore MacKinnon was very persistent in his exercises this morning. Besides zigzagging the ships were put through a long sound-signals exercise, and hooters were blowing all over the convoy from 10 a.m. to 11.30 a.m. It offered some passing entertainment, picking out which ship was blowing by the sound of her hooter. *Corinthic* had a good strong one which acted straight away and was quite definite . . . *Beatus*, next door to her, would do a 'sisssss' of varied length before she started to 'hooooo', while *Blairspey*, on the other side, made heavy weather of it with someone pulling the lanyard who took a long time over the dots and dashes. *Assyrina*'s hooter had a double note. Above them all sounded the posh modern hooter of the big French tanker.

Besides the hooter-blowing flag signals went up at frequent intervals, and there were many men who derived great interest from trying to learn the various flags.

Whether by good luck or good schooling, it was all a sight more orderly than on previous SC convoys, whose Commodores had wept in fury at the lackadaisical standard of the simplest flag signalling and roundly cursed the foreigners who could not - or would not - read semaphore. When, as on one well remembered occasion, two hoists from the International Code Book had taken three hours ten minutes to pass through a convoy, such anger was well justified. The Germans could have sunk them all in less than half the time.

But if he had achieved tolerable order among his flock, one failing that Commodore MacKinnon could not correct was the prolific smoke they made. It wafted upwards in a clear sky, a treat for enemy eyes. Steamers were made to steam, and testy signals of 'Make less smoke' brought little result from ships doing their best on poor quality coal. The *Assyrian* herself, denied her good Welsh coal, was just as guilty as the rest.

At noon the convoy, still maintaining a good seven knots, reached position 46 deg. 35 min. N, 49 deg. 13 min. W. They were beginning to rise sharply northwards now.

In the quiet of the afternoon crews prepared their 'sub bags' once again. These were the small canvas bags, like miniature kit-bags, into which each man packed his most valued personal possessions, all ready for the lifeboat. The lifeboats themselves were checked over and things generally got ready for entering the danger zone. Those ships which had guns made sure they were in working order. In convoy there could be no more practice, no more popping off at a barrel dropped overboard. The next shots, when fired, would be at the enemy.

Apart from these activities crews settled to the business of overcoming the feeling of tenseness coupled with sheer boredom which was the merchant seaman's lot for long, monotonous periods in convoy.

For most men that meant cards. Cards, whether played for money or matchsticks, was more than a relaxation, it was a kind of religion. And a special part of that religion was the game of cribbage. Once, not so long ago, aboard the newcomer, *Shekatika* when a great shout went up and the din and cheering was immense people rushed into the saloon thinking wildly that perhaps the Germans had given in. Not so. It was just that twenty-nine, the greatest score mathematically possible in the game of cribbage, and one almost impossible to achieve statistically speaking, had just turned up in the 'box' in a game of five card, four-handed crib.

There were other forms of recreation, too. Aboard *Assyrian* the three French sailors sat on a hatch singing happily along with 'Chippy', the young ship's carpenter from Anglesey. The Frenchmen and he had found to their delight that the songs of Brittany and Wales both had a Celtic origin and could be sung by either. Below, Second Engineer Bill Venables, when off watch, studied his notes on the Flying Flea he was making to the design of its inventor, Henri Mignet. Venables had been building the little aeroplane in his spare time for two years now. On other voyages he had completed the fuselage, rudder and framework of the wings, working in the space for'ard where the twin-screw *Assyrian*'s two shaft tunnels converged. It made an ideal workshop, though he had had to make the fuselage half an inch narrower than specification in order to get it through the tunnel door into the engine room. Back home in Liverpool he had a brand new 34 horse-power Anzani engine, and now he was saving money for the linen and dope for the wings . . . quite an item when as second engineer his wages came to only £17 10s a month. When war broke out he had transferred his dissembled Flea from the ship to his home, but he was still reluctant to relinquish his dream of building and flying his own plane, which he hoped to do when the war was ended. So he had spent a voyage designing and making a propeller of laminated beech and mahogany, which now hung over his bunk.

Yes, one day he would fly. Bill Venables was determined about that.

Wednesday, October 9. It was still gloriously fine and sunny, and everyone was astonished at the continued good weather. A little uneasy, too. Seas like this favoured a searching enemy, and there were a few quiet prayers offered that the weather would eventually revert to its normal stormy self, when the rough conditions would make it more difficult for a U-boat to find them.

The flag-painted Swedish ship had inexcusably shown a light during the night and was severely reprimanded by the Commodore. Blackout was very strict and most ships exercised their own discipline on this. Like on the *Corinthic*, where any light shown after blackout time was liable to cost a man a fine of five shillings. The long and lonely night hours were always a time of extra tension. Tell-tale sparks might suddenly come from the funnel . . . someone on deck might forgetfully light a match . . .

There were more manoeuvres this morning for over an hour as Commodore MacKinnon ran up his various flag commands. Everyone seemed to be performing pretty satisfactorily.

They were moving more sharply to the east now in their northerly climb. For the listening ships' radio officers this meant farther and farther away from the New World's cacophony of commercial radio and back into the bleak ocean area of monotonous morse navigation warning signals and the occasional faint yelp of hurried distress signals, which sometimes at night could be heard from thousands of miles away. Good-bye to all the cowboy songs . . . 'Ya gotta rope and throw, leave Oklahoma when the sun is low, if ya wanna be a cowboy . . .'

It was always a novel experience for merchant radio officers making their first trip out to Canada, accustomed only to the wartime diet of the BBC's Home and Forces programmes. On nearing Canada the background chatter of the radio networks would begin to break through on the ship's primitive two-valve set, pouring straight down the hundreds of feet of aerial wire and making raucous interference. Now, for SC7, the situation was in reverse, the aerials beginning to clear except for the last sounds of station VONF, Newfoundland, which often held the whiphand in the interference. Lone announcers on VONF held the fort for hours at a time, playing records, giving news of the twins just born up in the backwoods, and relaying sweetheart messages to men out fishing on the foggy Newfoundland Banks. A tune, a chat, and a bit of fun. Like the girl disc jockey who recited, apropos of nothing, between records:

'If a cargo ship, ten thousand tons,
Had sailed ten thousand miles,
With a cargo large of overshoes, and carving knives and files,
If all the mates were six feet tall,
The engineers the same,
Would you subtract or multiply to find the Captain's name . . .?'

Generally only the radio officers on their listening watch were treated to these delights, for the use of personal radios aboard ship by anyone was forbidden, such sets being either confiscated or dismantled for the duration of the voyage, though there were always some seamen who managed to hold on to their sets and have a listen in occasionally. It was questionable whether any

U-boat ever did home in on a ship or convoy through tracking a seaman's radio, but there was no doubt of the disturbing oscillations produced in the 160 metre trawler-band by the cheap superheterodyne radio sets.

The ships' own receivers were often just as guilty of oscillation, which was a far more serious problem. Commodores of earlier SC convoys had vigorously complained of W/T oscillation from ships, especially the foreigners, and urged that wireless cabins and sets should be sealed before sailing. On some earlier convoys many ships had had only one radio officer, which meant that sets could not be manned round the clock but only during the hours these officers were on watch. The result was that at certain watch commencement times, all sets were switched on at roughly the same moment. The discordant chorus of oscillating whistles and howls, grunts and groans on the air waves that followed could have alerted any listening U-boat and informed him of the coming-on-watch times. At least on SC7, with most ships having two radio officers, the watch was continuous and much of this row was avoided.

6 p.m. Clocks were advanced 30 minutes. The barometer was falling rapidly, and the wind had increased to Force 7 southerly, blowing a near gale. The longed for change in the weather had not been slow in coming.

And what was the radioed news from home, as against the sarcastic prattling of the traitorous Lord Haw-Haw?

The Germans were sweeping into Rumania . . . London had suffered its biggest night bombing raid yet, with very heavy casualties . . . the German invasion fleet was poised to strike. . . .

Thursday, October 10. The strong wind continued, and it began to rain. It pelted down all morning. The wind gathered force and ships were taking seas. As the going got more difficult they started to roll a good deal. One or two vessels, labouring heavily under the strain, began to lag behind, earning swiftly signalled rebukes from the Commodore.

The noon position was 51 deg. 47 min. N, 43 deg. 43 min. W. It had been a steep journey north, and now the convoy's path would taper into a more north-easterly curve, though as the voyage continued they would go still higher north to a point below Iceland, where, if a ruler were laid across the chart, they would be on a level with the Orkneys. But this would not be for another six days yet.

On they sailed, taking heavy seas consistently throughout a wild, uncomfortable night.

Friday, October 11. This morning the sun shone, but the heavy seas continued unabated. Decks ran with water as ships pitched and rolled, and breakfast was an adventure. The balancing of a cup of tea in one hand while manoeuvring curry on to a fork with the other, at the same time swaying sideways in rapidly alternating directions, was a very complicated operation.

The storm was in for the day, no doubt about it. The once calm, unruffled convoy presented a far different spectacle now. One minute ships rode right on the heights of the waves, and the next they had practically disappeared below them. It was impossible for the lookouts on any one ship to count more than about twenty other vessels in company. Several ships thrown out of formation by the rough seas of the night were struggling to regain their positions, but it seemed clear that others, noticeably the two Lakers, were no longer in sight.

After a flurry of signalling through the tossing ranks, Commodore MacKinnon and Commander Dickinson, in the attentive *Scarborough*, reached a final count of the ships in convoy, or at least in sight of it. Four vessels were missing: two big old Greek tramps, each well over three thousand tons, and the two Lakers.

The Greeks were *Niritos*, loaded with sulphur, and the *Aenos*, carrying grain. The Lakers were the *Trevisa* and the *Eaglescliffe Hall?*

All masters had been advised of the daily 'rendezvous' positions of SC7, so that they might hurry their way back to the convoy should they become detached from it in darkness or bad weather. Would these four storm-tossed absentees manage to fight their way back?

The two Greeks, perhaps. But the slow, erratic Lakers? At most it now seemed a faint hope.

4
The Luck of the Lakers

In the growing seas, the Laker *Trevisa* had fought a steadily losing battle. For most of the twenty-five years of her life she had been employed on the unadventurous routine duty of carrying coal between Lake Erie and Montreal, and her 1,800 tons were not designed to withstand the punishing Atlantic rollers.

While the weather was calm to moderate she had been able to keep up with the convoy, but she had no reserves in power or speed, and as the seas and weather worsened she dropped astern, the convoy drawing well ahead of her and finally vanishing over the horizon.

Left to struggle on alone in the heavy seas, *Trevisa*'s situation was not a pleasant one. She was a straggler, and everyone knew what happened to stragglers. Also, there was an additional factor which gave her crew cause for alarm.

Like all the Lakers the *Trevisa*, from Montreal, was being sailed to the U.K. by a British crew sent out specially to Canada to collect her. The officers in these crews stayed as a rule at the same hotel in Montreal while the boats were got ready and their engines adapted for salt water, and it was here that *Trevisa*'s officers had first become aware of their master's excessive liking for his liquor. The captain was in his fifties, and seemed to have acquired a lifetime's thirst. Nor did his drinking slacken off at all when they steamed down to the Bay of Fundy to collect their load of prepared spruce, intended for the construction of fighter aircraft. And once SC7 put to sea he went on the grog in earnest, being patently under the influence of liquor for more than half his waking hours.

Now, with the convoy out of sight, the master of the *Trevisa* ordered a change of course, and although his officers and most of the crew knew him to be still well in his cups, they expected him at least to be following the official instructions for stragglers which had been given to all the masters. And so the old Laker pushed her way onward at the best speed that her limited engine-power would allow.

As time went by, however, the *Trevisa*'s new course took her strangely farther south, and her officers grew worried. It was then discovered that instead of steering a course to pass between certain secret map reference positions set up across the North Atlantic, the captain was in fact steering a course to pass *through* the first of these reference points, and then presumably through all the others, one by one. It was a huge and totally unnecessary detour to make, if not an extremely foolish and dangerous one; but it was the master's decision, and as such could not be questioned.

On October 15, five days after losing the convoy, *Trevisa*, travelling far south of SC7's curving northerly route, neared 21 degrees West. This was the meridian that marked the outer limit of the Western Approaches - the farthest point in the Atlantic to which British warships came to shepherd in the homeward-bound convoys. But no escorts came this far south, more than 120 miles below the route of SC7.

As the old Laker plodded on over mile after mile of dangerous ocean Radio Officer Charles Littleboy was seized by a feeling of impending disaster and determined to do something about it. He made every possible preparation in the radio room to keep going in the case of a total power failure, and also rigged up an emergency light. At 9 p.m. on October 15 he went into the chartroom and, with the second mate's permission, estimated and drew up a list of *Trevisa*'s positions by latitude and longitude for every half hour during the coming night. He took the list down to the radio room and fastened it down beside the morse key. He then went to his cabin, which formed part of the radio room, and lay on his bed, fully dressed and wearing a partly inflated life-jacket. . . .

It was after two o'clock in the morning when, in the moonlight, U-124 came upon its prey. Kapitanleutnant Wilhelm Georg

Schulz could hardly believe his good fortune. A seasoned Atlantic commander, he was out on the twelfth day of his patrol from the U-boat base at Lorient. U-124, with Schulz's edelweiss emblem painted on its conning-tower, was one of the big new ocean-going U-boats with a surface speed of well over sixteen knots, and it was faster than *Trevisa*'s six or seven knots even when submerged. It carried twenty-two torpedoes, though for the curious looking ship which now laboured surprisingly across its path only one would be necessary.

However, Kapitanleutnant Schulz took no chances. He submerged and made a textbook attack. The torpedo sped to its target and struck with a great flash in the night. *Trevisa* seemed to disappear. Schulz marked 'Sunk' in his logbook, and U-124 continued on patrol.

The torpedo ripped into *Trevisa* and blew off the whole of her stern in a thousand flying fragments. The explosion disembowelled the engine-room, killing all the engine staff . . . the chief, second and third engineers, a donkeyman and a fireman. The ship's lifeboats were blown to bits and the vessel plunged into total darkness.

For Radio Officer Littleboy, who was lying on his bed when the torpedo struck, pressure seemed to predominate over noise. His body appeared to be held against the ceiling, but in the darkness it was impossible to identify walls, ceiling or floor, until gravity caused him to fall back to the sloping deck. He then saw faint moonlight coming through the open doorway and reasoned that the radio room was still right side up. Scrambling up and with the doorway to guide him, he quickly found and switched on the emergency light which he had prepared. It undoubtedly saved many lives, including his own.

Using the emergency power he started up the transmitter, suddenly remembered the radio antenna and dashed out on deck to find it still luckily in place with both masts nearly vertical, then ran back to the radio room, and without waiting for the captain's authority tapped out the distress signal '. . . SSSS . . .' together with his own estimate of the ship's position as shown by the list he had put ready. It was a good feeling to get an immediate answer from both sides of the Atlantic. He repeated the distress call several times, stressing the fact that *Trevisa* was turning over and sinking, firstly to give any nearby ship a chance to take radio bearings, and secondly to assure the U-boat that its job was completed - they didn't want a second torpedo. It was reassuring to hear a British coastal station speedily repeat his message on the distress frequency.

He then hurried back on deck. *Trevisa* was sinking slowly by her shattered stern and listing ominously as she made to turn over. There were just over a dozen survivors and only two rafts between them, primitive affairs consisting of four 40-gallon oildrums in a wooden lattice framework. Some men in their panic wanted to sit on the rafts and let the dying Laker sink beneath them, but Littleboy suggested they should carry the rafts to the water's edge and launch them properly. It would be safer and would keep them busy. All agreed to do this, and it was only when they tried to move the rafts that it was discovered they were both chained firmly to the deck. The horrible thought of what would have happened had they simply sat on them as the ship sank below the surface came as a cold douche upon fuddled minds.

Littleboy and the second mate now became aware of the curious absence of the captain and hurried to investigate. The mate led the way for'ard to the master's cabin, and there they found him in a drunken stupor, totally unaware that anything was wrong. They had to throw respect for authority to the winds and use considerable physical force to bring him round and get him on his feet. When the situation finally dawned on him he sobered up fast.

On returning to the deck Littleboy and the mate helped to release the first raft from its chain and launch it over the side. The first man to jump aboard was a frightened young seaman who immediately pushed it away from the ship and started to drift off to sea alone. It took much cajoling by the elderly chief officer to persuade him to paddle the raft back to the side of the listing ship, after which another seven men clambered on and the raft moved away fully loaded.

In the meantime the second mate had disappeared, so those remaining prepared to launch the second raft without his help. They had got the raft on to the sloping deck, ready to slip down into the water, when the mate reappeared. He had rushed to his cabin to pack his personal effects, and now arrived on deck humping two large suitcases, together with a typewriter tucked under one arm and the ship's chronometer under the other, and his pockets and clothing bulging with every possible domestic commodity other than food and water. In the midst of grave emergency he cut a tragically ludicrous figure, for there was no possible stowage space for any of his luggage aboard the raft.

But his foolishness did not justify the action that followed.

The bleary-eyed captain, taking the opportunity to perform his one and only authoritative act of the night, angrily snatched the baggage away from the second mate and hurled it piece by piece into the sea. It would have been easier for him to leave the pathetic load on deck and show a little consideration towards the man who had just helped to rouse him and save his life, but only now was the captain beginning to show any signs of command. He had taken no part in the abandon-ship routine nor given any orders about sending a distress message or disposing of the ship's secret code books. The radio officer had locked these books in the steel lockers of the radio room so that they would go down with the ship. The flimsy code 'key' sheet he kept in his pocket to hand to his captain later - if they survived.

By this time the ship's starboard rails were well under water and they had no difficulty in launching the second raft. The remaining six survivors who scrambled aboard it were the captain, chief officer, second mate, radio officer and two young seamen. They paddled the raft to a safe distance away from the overturning ship and waited. It was a strangely calm, moonlit night as they huddled there, gently, riding the slight swell, only the radio officer in uniform, the others wearing whatever clothes they had been able to grab in the emergency. At frequent intervals came the question, 'Did you get the distress message away, Sparks?' and repeatedly he assured them that the message had been sent and acknowledged. But what were their chances of being picked up? This question was not one to be debated, every man chewing it over to himself in agonised silence.

Then, just as dawn was breaking on the eastern horizon, there came the threat of high danger when the chief officer saw a vague shape in the distance. Everyone was convinced that it was the lurking U-boat, now moving in to spray the rafts with machine-gun fire, and they crouched down in fear. In a little while, however, what they had thought to be a conning-tower turned into a topmast and bridge - it was a British destroyer. Jubilantly the chief officer and second mate set off signal flares, and as the ship closed, the radio officer flashed a warning message with his torch . . . 'Sub near.' Within minutes the two rafts were being circled by three destroyers, one of which dropped speed and closed in alongside. It was HMS *Keppel?* 'Hurry, there! Hurry!' came the shouts from her bridge, and they lost no time in climbing up the scrambling nets lowered over the destroyer's side.

With all fourteen of them safely aboard, *Keppel* drew away from the scene, as did HMS *Sable*, leaving the third of the trio, the Canadian destroyer *Ottawa*, to stand by the now completely overturned and half sunken *Trevisa*. At 8.21 a.m. she wirelessed the Commander-in-Chief, Western Approaches: '*Trevisa* bottom up, 25 feet of her showing, five feet above water, propose to sink . . .' It did not take much effort from *Ottawa*'s gunners to send the Laker's remains sliding below the surface of the compassionate sea. She died in position 57.28N, 20.30W. For a quarter of a century she had hauled her cargoes round the sweet waters of the Great Lakes, now her distant grave was the deep mid-Atlantic. She took down with her six men.

Aboard *Keppel* the survivors were given a quick examination by the destroyer's doctor, who found no bones broken. The prescription was a hot bath and bed, *Keppel*'s officers and crew willingly doubling up to provide accommodation for them.

Saved, and comfortable . . . the idle unemployed. For as *Trevisa* sank, so did the jobs of her crew. Their term of engagement ended on October 16, 1940 at the hour the waves closed above her. In most ships perhaps one or two officers would remain on salary, but for the rest, and the seamen, the loss of their vessel rendered them unemployed and so unpaid.

Such were the unreasonable conditions under which Britain's merchant seamen at this time loyally fought the war.

On this same day, October 16, hundred of miles away to the north-east, the other Laker which had lost the convoy was still pressing on determinedly for the U.K.

The *Eaglescliffe Hall* was only half the age of *Trevisa* and at 1,900 tons was a hundred tons bigger, but her handicaps were much the same, if not greater. Her three-cylinder steam reciprocating engines were of a mere 81 horse-power. They had been designed to ease her over smooth inland waters, and the strain of keeping up with a seven-knot ocean convoy had finally proved too much. She gradually lost ground due to steering, engine and steaming difficulties, and in the end had just had to stop. By the time the trouble was cleared sufficiently for her to continue, the convoy had long disappeared.

On finding himself alone in mid-ocean without the remotest hope of catching up with SC7, Captain Charles Madsen followed his own counsel. Although only in his early forties, he was a well-experienced master who had sailed all kinds of general cargo ships all over the world, and what was more he knew the

North Atlantic like the back of his hand. In spite of all the dangers that ocean might now hold, he knew that with *Eaglescliffe Hall*'s severe limitations there was only one course of action for him to take, and that was to make his way home by the shortest route. Accordingly he laid course direct for the Butt of Lewis.

And so for five days now, since losing the convoy, *Eaglescliffe Hall* had pressed ahead, her dogged performance being something of a tribute to the Middlesbrough shipyard that built her back in 1928, and to her crew, mainly Tynesiders like their captain, who almost willed her through the waves.

Like *Trevisa!* the *Eaglescliffe Hall!* also a Montreal boat, was stacked to capacity with timber. Her sole armament consisted of a Thompson gun which had been delivered aboard in pieces at Sydney, together with a book of instructions on how to assemble the weapon, and a small amount of ammunition. By trial and error they had put the gun together, but a positive gnat's sting it seemed as they steamed on through dangerous seas.

Captain Madsen had not left the wheelhouse by day or night since leaving Sydney, nearly two weeks ago now. The dark early hours of October 17 found him there, keeping alert watch on the night sea, when suddenly he saw a mysterious craft low in the water and travelling at considerable speed pass by on *Eaglescliffe Hall*'s port side. It was a heart-stopping moment, for it could only have been a surfaced U-boat, racing along on its fast diesel engines. Yet the next anxious minutes brought no further sign of the marauder. To their immense relief either they had not been seen or the German had bigger fish to fry.

Shortly afterwards another traveller emerged out of the night, this time the solid dark shape of a large steamer,which overtook and passed the Laker on the starboard side. She was so close that in the moonlight Captain Madsen immediately recognized her as the *Aenos*, one of the two Greek vessels which, unknown to him, had also lost the convoy. He identified *Aenos* from her clipper stem, for the thirty-year-old ship was originally the *Cedar Branch*, built in Sunderland, and Captain Madsen had known her well before she was sold off to the Greeks.

Nearly twice the tonnage of the Laker, the more powerful *Aenos*, loaded with grain, steamed ahead into the night and was gone, leaving *Eaglescliffe Hall* to continue her lone passage.

The rest of the night passed quietly and dawn broke on an empty sea, but the mid-morning brought more company, this time in the sky. It was a patrolling plane from Coastal Command. Circling low, it began to blink out a message on its Aldis lamp . . . 'Lifeboats, rafts and men in distress 25 miles ahead . . .'

It was 10.20 a.m. Captain Madsen asked his chief engineer for every ounce of power, stretching *Eaglescliffe Hall*'s engines to their utmost speed of seven knots, and after three hours' hard steaming the Laker sighted two lifeboats, two rafts, and some miserable pieces of floating wreckage, all that remained of a big steamship of 3,500 tons. At 1.45 p.m. in position 58.56 N, 13.03 W she took aboard twenty-five shocked survivors of the ss. *Aenos*.

Captain Laskarides, very distressed, described as well as he could in broken English how his ship had been torpedoed, the explosion killing three men in the engine-room. After they had abandoned ship and the crippled *Aenos* showed no immediate signs of sinking, the U-boat had finished her off by gunfire. His ship went down at 8.30 a,m., and he and his men had been adrift for some five hours in the waterlogged lifeboats and on the rafts.

It seemed clear that *Aenos*'s killer was the U-boat which had sped past *Eaglescliffe Hall* during the night. The unfortunate *Aenos* had steamed on close behind it, right into the German's patrol area and into his waiting jaws. The U-boat, its job done, had obviously cleared away from the scene fast on sighting the patrolling aircraft. Had it not been for the timely presence of the plane, the Laker would without doubt have been the U-boat's next victim.

Fortune had smiled on them. After taking aboard the exhausted Greeks, Captain Madsen set course to pass outside the Hebrides for Barra Head, hoping to avoid the route of further trouble and in addition to make landfall nearer in case of accidents.

Held as they were in the gunsights of the Germans there had been no time for the Greeks to abandon ship with any ceremony, and they had only what they stood up in, together with a few valuables such as watches and money which they had carried on them at the time the ship was struck. They were in a state of acute shock and bewilderment that it could have happened to them, not seeming to have any notion what war conditions were. Their sole desire was to get as far away as possible from the scene of their encounter with the enemy.

As the Laker slowly ate up the miles they continued very jittery, peering anxiously ahead for the first sight of land. When at last it came, the faint outline of the rugged islands of St. Kilda, they nearly wept for joy. But on learning to their dismay that *Eaglescliffe Hall* did not intend to call there, their emotion knew no bounds. All they desperately wanted was to feel firm earth under their feet, far away from the waters which any minute might release another killer torpedo. A deputation begged Captain Madsen to put them ashore at St. Kilda. They did not seem to know or care that the austere islands were now totally unoccupied, the remaining few dozen inhabitants having been evacuated to the Scottish mainland, more than a hundred miles away, years earlier. The Laker's captain tried to explain to them that if he landed them there they would be in for a very long wait, quite apart from the serious problems of trying to keep themselves alive. His ship, he repeated, was bound for the Clyde.

At this many of the Greeks broke down and some openly sobbed. Through tears they pleaded with him that they could go no farther - that they were terrified that even now a U-boat might be shadowing them to send them to the watery grave from which they had only recently escaped. But Captain Madsen was adamant. It was to be the Clyde or the enemy, he told them. The ship would take her chance, and so must they. Sorrowfully they resigned themselves to this fact.

The master now grimly faced the last lap of his dangerous journey. *Eaglescliffe Hall*, he was determined, would bring herself, her crew and her load of survivors into Rothesay Bay intact.

Incredibly, her weird and wonderful engines responding gamely to the last calls made on them, the Laker did just that. At 10 p.m. on Saturday, October 19, 1940 she steamed safely in, alone and unheralded in the pitch dark blackout.

But next morning it was different. As she moved up from Rothesay Bay to Gourock pier she was greeted by rousing cheers and an exuberant fanfare of ships' hooters.

Too slow to get out of her own way? Slow, yes, but bloody sure!

5

The First of the Hunters

Saturday, October 12. Two days after the disappearance of the Lakers and the two Greeks, convoy SC7 forged on through heavy seas. Ships had tossed and rolled throughout the night, and so it continued for most of the morning, seamen holding on to any and everything as their vessels rode the boisterous Atlantic. In spite of the awkward conditions the Commodore still sent up many flag hoists, a number of vessels being ordered to change their positions and group up with others bound for the same final destinations.

During the afternoon the buffeting wind began to die down and progress became fairly comfortable again. Only a thousand-odd miles to go as the crow flies!

Sunday, October 13. It poured with rain, and the glass went down once more. But there was a cheering sun and they were managing a consistent seven knots now, after the previous day's struggle to keep at six knots. The noon position was 55.59 N, 32.48 W, and the convoy commenced zigzag No. 17. From tomorrow night they would be entering the high danger zone.

There was much speculation as to when ships would arrive at their various ports. The lucky ones were those that would end or break their journey at Rothesay, as against those bound for the east coast. The Rothesay ships should arrive late on Friday night or early Saturday morning. It depended on the weather, U-boats, enemy aircraft, and a few other minor details . . .

The convoy continued zigzagging throughout the night.

Monday, October 14. They were now less than 30 degrees West and into the straight for home. Metaphorically 'straight', for they were still furiously zigzagging, to the regular ten-minutely discomfort of everyone as each vessel rolled over on to her new course.

The wind was kinder, and a weak sun shone; only an occasional sea now flopped on to the deck.

Several of the timber ships had noticeably increased lists, but all vessels kept good station. The daily manoeuvres were carried out with an easy familiarity, flag signals going up with promptitude, and altogether *Assyrian*'s admiral had got them running in real Navy fashion.

They were farther north than ever now, having passed beyond 57. N, and were still climbing. Yet it was not too cold.

Tuesday, October 15. The convoy continued rising north towards Iceland, the weather beginning to feel like it. Both sky and sea were grey, and the wind had turned decidedly wintry. They were above 58 degrees North, and passing 25 degrees West.

The day brought a piece of good cheer. One of the four missing vessels had managed to rejoin. She was the Greek *Niritos*, carrying a cargo of sulphur. A typical sturdy, ageing old tramp was the *Niritos*. Greek she might be now, but she had started out as a British ship from West Hartlepool, three names and thirty-three years ago, back in 1907.

There was still no sign of the other missing Greek, *Aenos*, and the two Lakers. There was little hope felt of ever seeing them again now.

The convoy moved on steadily throughout the day, *Scarborough* retaining her pathfinding position ahead as though fastened by an invisible tie to the leader of each column of ships.

During the afternoon the Commodore made the warning signal: 'Keep sharp lookout for submarine astern.' They must be on their guard now for any shadowing U-boat.

In the evening zigzagging began again in complicated style. Shortly after midnight an outward-bound convoy passed by, faintly visible in the distance, steaming safely out of the danger zone SC7 was now entering. Ships that pass in the night . . .

*

Wednesday, October 16. It was a pleasantly sunny morning, though with the wind very cold, but aboard the *Assyrian* and other ships which had picked up the distress message, they knew that the crew of the *Trevisa* would not be thinking much about the weather or anything else, for she had been torpedoed far to the south. Sadly, some radio officers did not even recognize the name or call sign as being that of one of the lost Lakers, it remained just one more distress call among several heard during the night. But in *Assyrian* they knew it only too well. With mixed feelings Commodore MacKinnon took up his list of ships and struck off *Trevisa*'s name. She was the first convoy vessel he had lost through enemy action. There had to be a first victim, and he had been prepared for it each time he sailed, but now that it had happened it was none the easier to accept. Each ship, even the dirtiest and most troublesome tramp, was a living thing, besides being of great need to Britain's war effort, and *Trevisa*'s crew were not just another cold statistic but a company of human individuals. What had been their fate?

At noon the convoy reached its highest point on the chart, 59.31 N, 21.39 W. From now on its path would follow a steady curve to the south-east, advancing east much more rapidly than on the climb to the north.

Late in the afternoon a lone ship hove into sight, travelling far over on the port side of the convoy. As she steamed abeam of them the end of a rainbow showed immediately behind her. A strange, enchanting spectacle, it probably would have been regarded as an omen of something or other by superstitious seamen of bygone days.

And then suddenly there was a signal lamp flashing to the north, and as the dying rays of the sun moved slowly across the horizon, crews were relieved and pleased to see the silhouettes of two small warships coming to meet them. Were they guardian ships of the Northern Patrol, or the convoy's long awaited escort?

They were not left in doubt for very long.

The sloop HMS *Fowey* and corvette HMS *Bluebell* had anticipated meeting up with SC7 soon after 9 p.m., but instead both sighted the convoy at 6 p.m. They therefore decided to leave the outward-bound convoy they had been helping to escort, and join SC7 immediately.

Under the orders of Commander Dickinson in *Scarborough* each now took up their escort positions. *Scarborough* herself moved to the port wing of the convoy. *Fowey* took the starboard wing, and *Bluebell* went astern.

It was a cheering sight for the merchantmen, now at least the convoy could show a few teeth. But they might not have been quite so pleased had they known that *Fowey* already carried a large quota of survivors. They were the entire crew of the New Zealand Shipping Company's big 9,000-ton steamer *Hurunui*, which had been torpedoed and sunk two days earlier on the outward convoy. Some of these men now stood on *Fowey*'s deck and looked on apprehensively as she joined SC7. They had just escaped a watery tomb and now here they were, having to sail back again over each dangerous mile.

Fowey was about the same size as *Scarborough*. She had been launched the same year, too, in 1930, but unlike *Scarborough* she had not been adapted for surveying but was designed to serve the multi-purpose role of escort sloop, minesweeper and admiral's yacht. Her pleasurable peacetime occupation had been that of generally showing the flag as a gunboat in the Persian Gulf. War had brought her to the Atlantic.

Camouflaged, and with four-inch guns fore and aft, *Fowey* looked a very purposeful ship. But it was always a surprise for others to see the pennant on her side, painted large and clear - 'U-15'. More than that, a first sight of it often made hearts jump for a painful second or two. It was easy to understand how already one merchant ship had rammed the sloop in error for a U-boat. Those responsible for the 'U' marking of some warships seemed to have little idea of the instant suspicion if not terror it could create in the minds of seamen, especially among harassed ships in darkness or bad weather.

The *Bluebell* was quite a different vessel. She was a corvette, only five months old, one of the new and strange breed of warship now beginning to make their mark in Atlantic escort work. The corvettes were in fact a development of the trawler, and had been intended for use as coastal escorts, but because of the desperate shortage of ocean escorts they were pitched almost at once into work for which they had never been designed - 'Cut off by the yard like a string of sausages', as one naval critic wryly observed. It made one dizzy to watch the corvettes in heavy seas. Like the trawlers they did not cut through the waves but rode over them. They bobbed and weaved, sat on the tops of waves, spun round like corks and generally bounced about in an alarming manner. But, overgrown trawlers as they might be, the corvettes could withstand exceptionally bad seas. Rather smaller than the sloops, they were very manoeuvrable and could reach a speed of fifteen knots. *Bluebell* had a four-inch gun, Lewis guns and, importantly, the latest type of asdic set, as against the earlier t[illegible]ted in *Fowey*.

There was another great difference between *Fowe*[illegible]d *Bluebell*. While the sloop was commanded by a naval lieutenant-commander, with a largely naval crew, *Bluebell*'s commander was a Merchant Navy officer of the Royal Naval Reserve, and her crew mostly inexperienced hostilities-only ratings. The fact that Lieutenant-Commander Robert Aubrey, RN, of *Fowey* and Lieutenant-Commander Robert Evan Sherwood, RNR, of *Bluebell* had never even met, meant little. The commanders of Western Approaches escorts at this time more often than not were complete strangers to each other. There had been no special training in working together against U-boats and there were no common plans of action. All escorts worked independently. They would accompany an outgoing convoy, then receive wirelessed instructions from Western Approaches Command, in Liverpool, to detach and rendezvous with an incoming convoy at a certain position, and escort it in. Off they went and if they were lucky they found the convoy - if by the time they arrived it had not moved to another position. They never knew which other warships, or how many, they would meet on the same mission. As they arrived singly at the convoy the escort senior to the others would assume authority and position them, and the command could be always changing with the arrival of a more senior ship.

So in the later hours of October 16 the two newcomers settled in with SC7 for the homeward run. To them it was just one more convoy among many, they had brought one out and now they were bringing one in, and the cycle would be repeated again and again, until they were deemed to have earned a break. Their duties with SC7 would last a bare four days and nights, during which time they would hardly get to know the name of a single ship. That is how it was, and there was no reason to suppose that this convoy of slow and aged ships would be any different.

Each of the new arrivals was a reflection of the character of her commander, both of whom had, in their respective ways, chosen the sea as a career at a very early age.

Fowey's Lieutenant-Commander Aubrey was a skilled naval officer of thirty-one, well-built and broad-shouldered, with plenty of drive and determination. He had entered the Royal Naval College at Dartmouth and first gone to sea in 1926. He had come to *Fowey* from commanding a destroyer flotilla leader, and had already seen plenty of action, including the Norwegian campaign. He was the type of man, a dedicated naval officer, who drew an easy respect from his juniors, even when they disagreed with some of his personal views. They counted their time with him as valuable experience.

Aubrey was a 'salt-horse' and disdainful of specialists, especially as to their ability in ship-handling. He was a prodder, a fighter, a man of swift, decisive action. Every forenoon his officers would be summoned to the boatdeck which he was pacing to 'tell the story of their lives,' which meant telling him what they had been doing so that he could find out those things they had not done. His terse comments would remain with them always . . . 'Procrastination is the thief of time' . . . 'Never volunteer any information' . . . 'I wouldn't know - I haven't taken a course' . . . 'How *right* are you?' . . . 'I don't give a fish's tit' . . . Blunt and pugnacious, but always fair was Aubrey, and as jolly as he could be assertive. He delighted in singing Frances Day songs such as 'Blue Champagne' and 'I'm just a little girl lost in a fog . . . Me and my dog, lost in a fog . . . Won't some kind gentleman see me home' . . . when his jowelly face would wreath in smiles as he beat time on his thighs.

Bluebell's Lieutenant-Commander Sherwood, RNR, stocky, bearded and bright-eyed, was the son of a merchant captain. Aged thirty-three, he began his apprenticeship at sea at the age of fifteen, and went on to become mate and then master in various East Coast vessels. Then, from 1935 onwards, he progressed from junior officer to master on the Holyhead-Dublin steamers.

On the outbreak of war Sherwood commanded trawlers on the Dover Patrol. He left Dover in May, 1940 to stand by *Bluebell* as she was being built, one of the very first of the new corvettes. He was then called to Dunkirk, as so many were, to join in the rescue work, and captained a tug which saved hundreds of exhausted soldiers from the beaches and brought them safely to Ramsgate. He returned to the Clyde to find *Bluebell* launched, and commissioned her in late August. Though the corvette had since been active for only two months she had seen plenty of sea time. After a week's 'work-up' at the battle school at Tobermory she had begun escorting convoys from Methil up round the north of Scotland into the Atlantic, and was then switched to Liverpool to escort outward-bound convoys and bring in the homecoming ones.

Sherwood never left *Bluebell*'s bridge, sleeping there in a hammock in the asdic house. He was a quick and confident commander, as well as displaying a keen sense of humour. He certainly needed to keep tight hold of the reins, for unlike the sloop, whose company was composed mostly of Naval Regulars, *Bluebell*'s crew were pretty raw. For three-quarters of them, conscript seamen ratings fresh from training school, *Bluebell* was their first ship - the first time they had ever been to sea. A handful of experienced A.B.s and petty officers, among them the coxswain, a recalled naval pensioner, served to inspire the rest. As for the officers, *Bluebell*'s number one was an RNVR lieutenant whose pre-war experience had consisted chiefly of yachting round the East Coast, while the two juniors, both Canadians, were young RCNVR sub-lieutenants only just out of training college.

Fowey and *Bluebell*. Apart from the Commodore ship and *Scarborough*, no other vessels in the convoy were yet aware of their names. But they would be, soon enough.

Thursday, October 17. In the old *Corinthic*, Second Radio Officer Henry Simpson, a nineteen-year-old from Aberdeen, was on listening watch in the dead hours after midnight. He had considerable misgivings about his date. His previous trip to sea had been for a few days only, when his ship was torpedoed - on the 17th. Indeed, the figure seemed to haunt him. He had joined the shipping company on April 17, been torpedoed on July 17, and signed on with the *Corinthic* on August 17. Now, in the early hours of another 17th, he was full of forebodings. He had been nervy all the previous evening, and hesitated a long time before turning in, even with all his clothes on, the practice they had been following for the past few days.

Just before Henry came on watch at midnight, First Radio Officer Kenneth Howell had picked up a distant message warning of a U-boat far ahead, and he half-jokingly told the mournful Henry to have a special listen-out at about 3 a.m., for he had worked out speeds and distances and thought perhaps the German might come their way.

As the convoy steamed silently on through the occasionally moonlit night, Henry Simpson sat glued to the radio, like his counterparts in the other merchant vessels, while men off-watch dozed fitfully on their bunks. From every bridge, eyes searched the fluctuating darkness. The weather remained clear with very good visibility, and the night clouds gradually dispersed to bathe the convoy in the light of a bright full moon.

It was a silent, almost mesmeric scene for the ships' lookouts, the convoy moving alone through the still night sea. But they were not alone. Unknown to them the first of the hunters had arrived. On its conning-tower, the emblem of an arched cat with glowing eyes. Waiting to pounce . . .

In the early hours of darkness before midnight U-48, a big new ocean-going boat commanded by Kapitanleutnant Heinrich Bleichrodt, had cruised easily over the surface of the fairly gentle sea, enjoying the welcome break in the weather after a stormy north-wester. The watch on the bridge could move around freely without lifebelts, looking poetically on the white horses of the sea shimmering in the silvery moonlight; the mood was rather that of an unhurried night-ride on peacetime manoeuvres rather than a wartime patrol searching for the enemy convoy lanes. But in a fraction of time all that was changed.

'Shadow in front!' went the message to the U-boat's commander. After only a few seconds on the bridge Kapitanleutnant Bleichrodt saw that there were indeed several small shadows ahead to starboard. He brought the U-boat full speed ahead closer to the shadows, and ordered the crew to battle stations. The first officer of the watch and the battle watch on the bridge took their positions. All could now see that they were in the presence of a considerable convoy. They counted more than thirty ships. The columns of smoke from the convoy formed avenues of poplars in the night sky.

Bleichrodt manoeuvred the U-boat still nearer to the convoy, and the Germans could then make out the shapes of the escort vessels. Bleichrodt turned the U-boat on to a parallel course, so as not to be seen and driven away. He then made U-48 follow all the movements of the convoy; its zigzag course was logged, and they were very soon able to establish its general eastward course and speed.

The glad tidings were wirelessed to the U-boat base at Lorient: U-48 had sighted a large convoy at map reference AL3388, heading East at seven knots.

Meanwhile they had been noting the movements of the three escorts. One (*Scarborough*) steamed on the port wing and ahead of the convoy, another (*Fowey*) patrolled the starboard wing, and the third vessel (*Bluebell*) was on station astern, as 'sweeper'. U-48 was in a favourable position, having the convoy and its protecting vessels between itself and the moon. The silhouettes of the ships were clearly visible, while the small shape of the U-boat would be hard to make out against the dark horizon.

Bleichrodt now had the task of bringing his U-boat into a

surface aiming position without being seen. He could only manage this when *Scarborough* was at her farthest point to starboard on her sweep ahead, and *Bluebell*, similarly, was sweeping to starboard astern, thus leaving the port wing temporarily unguarded; but every time U-48 tried to steer in towards its goal one of these two escorts would change course and come steaming back, causing the U-boat to turn quickly in order to avoid detection.

Bleichrodt could not wait much longer; once dawn came he would have to withdraw, as he could only continue to shadow the convoy during daylight by remaining outside the range of visibility. He was quietly cursing his luck when suddenly, with both escorts steaming to starboard, the opportune moment came. He passed a message to his crew: 'Attacking enemy convoy. Firing three-pronged blast.'

U-48 now moved in on the convoy's port bow, heading for the first column of ships. They went in slowly, for Bleichrodt did not want to betray his presence by the strong phosphorescence of the water churned up by the screw. The first officer of the watch was ordered to aim three torpedoes at three different vessels, which overlapped one another in their staggered course so that they appeared like one huge vessel.

The convoy loomed up in the moonlight until they were about three-quarters of a mile away from the target ships. Bleichrodt ordered the first officer to fire, and swung the boat over to starboard. All three torpedoes left their tubes smoothly and headed silently for their targets. U-48 then retreated in a north-westerly direction, first at low speed then at full speed ahead. The stopwatches of the first officer and first mate would tell them when the 'eels' should have reached their destinations.

Scarborough and *Bluebell* had by now changed course and were steaming back to the exposed port side of the convoy. Tense moments followed for the U-boat's crew. Would the torpedoes hit their mark? And would U-48 be far enough out of danger when they did?

Then they saw flames shoot up from the convoy and shortly afterwards heard in quick succession two dull detonations roll across the sea.

Kapitanleutnant Bleichrodt gave the order for emergency speed, it was imperative that he should get clear of the scene and back into the protective night shadow. The U-boat's radio operator was picking up strong distress signals on the 600-metre waveband, but because of the suddenly busy air waves it was not possible to make out from which ship or ships the signals were coming. Standing on the bridge of the U-boat, Bleichrodt had to keep warning his men to pull their eyes away from the flare-lit convoy and search the dark areas of the sea for a possible pursuer . . .

It was exactly 4 a.m. when the first of U-48's torpedoes struck home. There was a loud explosion astern of *Corinthic* . . . and then, almost before anyone could scramble up on deck, another explosion as fierce as the first. Immediately the unsleeping Commodore made the light signal from *Assyrian* for an emergency turn to starboard, and all ships wheeled away from the direction of the attack.

Two of U-48's torpedoes had found their targets. The first struck the great tanker *Languedoc* and sent her reeling.

In the Vice-Commodore ship *Scoresby*, forward and to starboard, they saw the brilliant orange flash of the explosion on *Languedoc* and the second mate called Captain Lawrence Zebedee Weatherill to the bridge. Below, Chief Officer Ronald Coultas sprang from his bunk the second he heard the explosion. He had just put one foot outside the saloon entrance preparatory to climbing the makeshift ladder which would allow him to see over the top of the great stack of pitprops on deck, and the captain had only that moment reached the bridge, when the second torpedo struck - blasting full into *Scoresby*'s side. It exploded in No. 3 hold aft of the engine-room, starting to flood it immediately, and rocked the teetering stacks of pitprops, which started to move dangerously, threatening the safety of the men aft. The ship's after end was sinking into the sea and after a speedy check of the damage there was no doubt that she had received a fatal hit.

Scoresby's captain and the entire ship's company made their way to the boats and all four lifeboats, still thankfully intact, were launched successfully in the light wind and moderate swell. Shortly before the master got into the last of the boats *Scoresby* began to sink by the stern.

Less than five minutes after the boats had drawn away the dying steamer reared her suffering bulk up to an almost vertical position and slid back until only her forecastle head was above water. For another three or four minutes she hung there, then suddenly she was gone, leaving only a mass of swirling pitprops and wreckage to mark her grave.

Languedoc's crew, too, had managed to get their boats away without mishap after first sending up a distress rocket. But their stricken ship still remained afloat.

Fowey, stationed two and a half miles from the convoy on its starboard side, heard the two explosions over the asdic, saw the distress rocket shoot up into the sky and the convoy make its emergency turn to starboard. It was clear the enemy attack had come from the port side, where *Scarborough* would be in need of assistance. Commander Aubrey increased his sloop's speed to her full fouteen knots, steamed round the rear of the convoy and took up station one mile on the starboard beam of the searching *Scarborough*. Together the two sloops, in company with *Bluebell*, which had steamed up from astern, now began an exhaustive moonlight hunt up the port side of the convoy, but it was entirely fruitless. Where the attacking U-boat had vanished to was a complete mystery, for none of the ships could gain an underwater contact.

Scarborough signalled *Bluebell* by dimmed morse lamp to return and pick up survivors while she and *Fowey* continued the search. None of the merchant ships had stopped to help the men from the torpedoed ships. Such action was considered too dangerous and was strictly forbidden by Defence of Merchant Shipping orders.

An hour after the attack the green light showed at *Assyrian*'s masthead and the convoy swung back on course, ships which had dispersed now rejoining, until once again the body of ships were proceeding in near perfect formation.

Bluebell, meanwhile, had gone off to hunt in the dark for the survivors, keeping a wary lookout for signs of the enemy. While the corvette was searching in the vicinity of the still floating *Languedoc* some shells whistled alarmingly over her. There was no evidence as to who it was who fired, it could have been any frightened merchantman, but whoever was the culprit the shots were too damned close. Eventually *Bluebell* found the French tanker's crew in their boats, scrambling nets were thrown down over the side and they were helped aboard. The corvette then continued her search for the survivors of *Scoresby?*

It was just before daylight when she located them, and it was an astonishing sight that met the eyes when the corvette drew near to the lifeboats, for all around the four boats there appeared to be a great black mass on the surface of the sea. As *Bluebell* drew closer still they were aware of a strange squelching noise rising from the black mass, an eerie sound quite unlike anything they had ever heard before. Commander Sherwood decided to keep clear of the spot till daylight, so that he could see what he was up against. It was a wise decision, for as dawn broke he discovered that the black mass was a huge cluster of pitprops disgorged by the torpedoed ship; they were moving up and down in the water, creating an odd squeaking noise as wood rubbed on wood. Wires which had been used to secure the pit-props on deck were now streaming among them in the sea and could have put *Bluebell* out of action had they fouled her propellers.

Sherwood manoeuvred the corvette carefully in and took the survivors aboard, all being safe and well. Never would he forget the eye-opening sight of *Scoresby*'s master coming aboard from his lifeboat, a very tall and handsome man, imposing in stature, and dressed in quite the most beautiful new uniform *Bluebell*'s commander had ever seen in his life! The explanation was that after giving the orders to take to the boats Captain Weatherill went into his quarters, put on his new uniform jacket, gathered an attache case containing the ship's papers and discharge books, also some loose clothing, and threw them down to the port side bridge lifeboat before going over to the starboard boat.

Bluebell now closed the crippled *Languedoc*. Although the tanker was very low in the water there still seemed to be half a chance of saving her, so her master, Captain Thompson, rowed over to the ship with his chief officer, second engineer, and some of the crew. But it did not take them long to discover that the engines could not be restarted, and that her hull was so damaged and open to the sea that it was only a matter of time before she sank. Until she did so she was a hazard to shipping, so *Bluebell* fired a few rounds from her four-inch into her, and as she was then obviously sinking, left her.

Bluebell now set out to catch up with the convoy, which had pulled away in the darkness hours ago. The seventy survivors she now carried well outnumbered her own ship's company of fifty-six and it was becoming more than a little crowded. . . .

While *Bluebell* was busy at her rescue work the two sloops had continued the hunt for the U-boat, but still without success. *Scarborough* then rejoined the convoy, leaving *Fowey* to carry on with the search for a time, but *Scarborough* had hardly regained her station when a Sunderland flying boat loomed out of the morning sky and flashed a message that it had sighted and attacked a U-boat a few miles to the north-west of the convoy. The time was 7.30 a.m.

It *had* to be SC7's attacker, and now that the aircraft had forced it to submerge there was every chance of moving in to the kill. Commander Dickinson made a rapid decision. *Bluebell* and *Fowey* would both be rejoining the convoy within a few hours and other escorts were expected, also there had been no wireless signals warning of U-boats anywhere near the convoy's route. So Dickinson turned his sloop, intent on putting paid to SC7's shadower.

After U-48's safe withdrawal to westwards from the convoy Kapitanleutnant Bleichrodt ordered his men to stand down from battle stations and the cook to give everybody a good breakfast. Bleichrodt decided that his best plan now was to shadow the convoy from a distance and keep reporting on it, as U-48 had only three torpedoes left, with only two of these usable. The U-boat's course of action during the daylight hours therefore seemed assured, when suddenly their plans were shattered.

Bleichrodt was standing on the bridge when it happened.

'Aircraft ahead!' shouted the second officer.

Bleichrodt gave the order to dive, and the men of the bridge watch sprang into the turret hatch. He was the last to go in, and as he did so he saw the Sunderland flying low towards them, already very close, winging in out of the early morning sky like a prehistoric monster after its prey.

'Depth regulator hard down!'

After some fifteen to eighteen seconds they had reached a depth of ten fathoms, and Bleichrodt was turning the handle of the turret hatch still tighter when the Sunderland hit them. Two bombs exploded so close to U-48 that it seemed as though a giant was shaking them in his mighty fist; the lights went out and water rushed through the hatches into the boat. The dials of the pressure gauge burst. The steep angle of dive caused everything that was not fixed to the bulkheads or deck to come crashing down and roll about. The crew had to cling on at their battle stations to prevent themselves being tossed forward. Bleichrodt took such a knock on his hands that he could not feel them, nor his arms, for some time; they hung lifeless at his sides. Wrapped in darkness, U-48 continued its headlong dive.

'Keep your heads,' Bleichrodt calmly told his men, and ordered the first engineer to continue diving still faster to 450 feet. 'Standby lighting.' It took a little time before the dim light from the emergency system was switched on.

Then came the Sunderland's second attack. First, the U-boat's operator on listening-post duty reported bombs hitting the surface of the water, then the boat was rocked by two waves of detonations. This time, however, they had reached a good depth and suffered no damage.

The boat's descent was arrested at 550 feet and it was then righted. The flooding flaps were closed. Bleichrodt gave the order to start the bilge pumps and clear up the mess in the boat as soon as U-48 was on even keel. The crew were well experienced and it did not take long for them to repair the damage, though it was impossible to right the gyro-compass. The leakage of water in the conning-tower sprang from the periscope gaskets, which had been holed by the pressure waves and were letting in water.

The Sunderland's crew had done their job well. The first bombs must have been planted just where U-48 had dived, and detonations just in front of the conning-tower. Had they landed on the bridge it would have been all up with them.

Bleichrodt could now feel his hands and arms coming back to life. He gave the order to proceed at half-speed submerged, steering westwards to get further away from the scene of the aircraft's attack. He intended to stay underwater for another hour and then surface to approach the convoy again.

The cook had just received orders to distribute the breakfast interrupted by the bombing, when a report came through from the radio room: 'Direction sounding aft. Propeller noise, turning fast, coming close at speed.'

Bleichrodt rushed into the radio room and jammed the headphones on his ears. The propeller noise could be clearly heard, and there was no mistaking that it came from a warship and not a merchantman. He realized at once what it meant. The Sunderland had reported to the escort vessels that it had driven U-48 below the surface. Now he would have to reckon with a depth-charge attack - and by how many vessels? He ordered the U-boat's engines to be set at crawling speed and called for strict silence in the boat. The dydrophones then told them that the searching vessel had slackened speed and finally stopped altogether, listening. Warning the crew to expect a depth-charge assault he sank the boat to 600 feet. The bilge pumps had to be started up again, for it was necessary at such a depth to ensure that the boat was not over-heavy. But in spite of the need to get rid of the water, after a time he ordered the pumps to be switched off again as they were making too much noise.

All remained quiet, and they could only sit and wait. At times like these, when being pursued by surface vessels, Bleichrodt's station was always by the dished bulkhead dividing the control room from the radio room. He sat there, with one foot in the radio room and one foot in the control room, able to watch both the radio operator and the depth regulator. All orders and reports were now passed in whispers or signs. The crew sat or squatted at their posts. The officers and petty officers were all positioned so that they could see their commander and watch for his signals.

For a time it seemed that U-48 might not be detected. Then, 'Surface vessel approaching to port.' Now everyone could hear the noise of the propellers even without headphones. All waited for the signal of a hand being dropped . . . and it was, six times. *Scarborough* had fired a pattern of depth-charges.

Aboard U-48 a stop-watch timed the depth charges to work out the depth at which they were set to explode. From the time *Scarborough* went over to top speed ahead, Bleichrodt did the same with U-48, turning away from his pursuer at 90 degrees. The essential thing was to get the U-boat out of the line of fire, even if it was only a few yards. One after another, as they had been discharged, the depth-charges went off with a great rumbling explosion which shook the U-boat but without causing any damage. All the charges were over their heads; the stop-watch indicated that they had been set to go off at depths between 250 and 450 feet.

When the explosions had died away Bleichrodt brought U-48's revs down again to crawling speed There then followed another long wait as *Scarborough* began listening and sounding once more. Then, again, another pattern of depth-charges, with the U-boat following the same tactics as before.

All through the morning and into the afternoon *Scarborough* harried U-48, losing contact, regaining it, attacking, and then losing contact once more. Meanwhile the convoy had sailed on far ahead. *Fowey* hurried to rejoin it and caught up with the columns of ships at 3.15 p.m. When *Bluebell* also rejoined a few hours later Commander Aubrey, now the senior escort, stationed the corvette on the port side of the convoy and steamed *Fowey* across to the starboard side. Both escorts kept a constant listening watch on the asdic, but through the afternoon and evening and into the first night hours, all remained quiet and uneventful. Mile by mile, SC7 drew nearer home. They passed 15 degrees West, following a course that would take them north of Rockall, the bare upthrust of rock 200 miles from the Hebrides.

For *Scarborough*, left far to the rear, it had been a frustrating day as she kept after the U-boat, playing a long game of cat and mouse and refusing to give best to her quarry. For more than eight hours U-48 was unable to get properly clear of the tirelessly searching sloop; the most Kapitanleutnant Bleichrodt could do was to manoeuvre the U-boat yard by yard outside of *Scarborough*'s area of search, hoping that she would at last give up and return to the convoy. Their good luck lay in the fact that none of the sloop's depth-charges came lower than about 400 feet; had they done so it could have been a very different story.

Finally their pursuer seemed to lose contact entirely; there were no more detonations, no more propeller noises. But Bleichrodt did not yet dare to surface. How often had it happened that searching warships had just stopped engines and waited, after their depth-charges were exhausted, until a U-boat was forced by shortage of oxygen or weak batteries to surface, when they moved in to the kill with their guns, or rammed the boat. He decided he would have to remain submerged until dusk at the very earliest; he must err on the side of safety.

When still no more depth-charges came the tension eased a little. Someone started to grumble that he was hungry, and everyone relieved their feelings in laughter. Bleichrodt had to warn his crew to silence again, although he did not find this easy. Eventually the ventilators were switched on and the foul air whipped into motion. Now at last the cook was able to serve up fresh coffee, and life came back into wan faces. Bleichrodt let the boat rise to 200 feet and every arrangement was made to surface; he felt it was high time that everyone should be freed from the long day's tension, not to mention certain human needs. While the U-boat was submerged the lavatory was out of use, and they had to resort to a couple of buckets placed in a corner of the control room near the periscope shaft, where they could do their business undisturbed. No one had had a warm meal since the midnight soup of the previous night, before the attack on the convoy; events since then had interrupted their meals. Now the crew's favourite dinner was ordered: rice soup with beef.

As night fell, U-48 went up to periscope depth. The guncrew stood ready in the control room, the munition store was opened, the escape apparatus checked, and the security arrangements for destruction of the boat in an emergency were gone over. All waited as Bleichrodt scanned the horizon. He trained the periscope all round and saw nothing. Extending the periscope further, he searched again, but still saw nothing but the shadows over the sea. He gave the order to surface. The boat gave a slight shudder and pushed its way yard by yard out of the water until it broke surface. Bleichrodt opened the hatch and entered the conning-tower alone, drawing air greedily into his starved lungs. When he had made quite sure that U-48 was alone, he ordered the diving cells to be blown out with the diesel engines until the boat was right out of the water.

The bridge watch was set up and U-48 began its surface voyage again. The batteries were recharged. One by one, men were allowed on to the bridge to fill their lungs with good air. . . .

Elsewhere in the night steamed *Scarborough*, still searching for her elusive foe. Grimly through the night hours she continued to search, her reward coming next morning, October 18, when U-48 was sighted on the surface far away. *Scarborough* immediately gave chase and fired her old four-inch gun, but the German was well out of range. And this time, U-48 had no need to submerge. As the sloop crammed on all speed in an all-out effort to overtake it, or at least come within firing range, the U-boat struck westward, showing a derisory clean pair of heels. It was a good three or four knots faster than its aged adversary and the distance between them increased to a hopeless expanse of ocean.

Despondently, Commander Dickinson abandoned the chase, and in the early afternoon set off after the convoy at *Scarborough*'s maximum speed of 14 knots. His efforts seemed to have been entirely wasted, and worse still, at this speed he had little hope of ever catching up with the convoy again.

In fact he would not, but neither would U-48, much to the disappointment of the German U-boat command. When Bleichrodt had signalled his discovery of the convoy to the U-boat base at Lorient, instructions had speedily gone out to five other U-boats operating to the east and north of Rockall to converge upon the convoy. It was confidently expected that U-48 would continue to shadow SC7 and report its course, so leading the other U-boats straight to it. But *Scarborough*'s relentless pursuit of U-48 had ruined everything, preventing Bleichrodt from ever finding the convoy again.

The German command had no knowledge of SC7's actual route, so at U-boat headquarters now the vexed question was: how can we re-establish contact with the lost convoy? The man who came up with the simple but effective answer was the Commander-in-Chief U-boats, Admiral Doenitz.

6

The Wolves Gather

Admiral Karl Doenitz, master-mind of the German U-boat Arm, had now reached the position in the sea war towards which he had been working since hostilities began. He commanded sufficient U-boats in the North Atlantic to deploy them in attacking groups - or 'wolf-packs' as they were soon to become known.

At the start of the war Germany possessed only fifty-seven U-boats, many of these of a small type, and during the first nine months there had been many calls on them for service in different areas of operation, including the Norwegian campaign. Even now, because of losses cancelling out the increasing numbers being built, the total number of U-boats had scarcely changed. But the summer of 1940 had seen more of the new big ocean-going boats coming into commission, fast, modern craft with a deadly torpedo load, and commanded by men whom Doenitz had been training from the mid-1930s for this eventuality. Now, greater efforts were being made in the North Atlantic, with damaging results for Britain.

It was Doenitz's firm, unswerving belief that the surest and quickest way for Germany to win the war was by cutting Britain's Atlantic lifeline. And this job, he was convinced, could best be done by U-boats, rather than by marauding warships.

As Captain Karl Doenitz he had been a U-boat 'ace' of World War I. Now, in supreme command of U-boat operations, he brought to the sea battle all his wealth of experience, plus carefully evolved plans which had been well tested over the past five years.

Doenitz, born of an old Prussian family, had entered the Imperial German Navy in 1910. He was twenty-three years old when the Kaisers' war began, and at the end of it was a seasoned campaigner of twenty-seven. Now, fighting Hitler's war, he was still only forty-eight, in the prime of active command, and the lessons he had learned from the last war were to be exploited to the full by his protégé commanders.

In particular, Doenitz had long reached the conclusion that success for the U-boats lay in attacking convoys not singly, but in strength. In 1914-18 this was impossible, a situation dictated by the primitive wireless equipment available. Communications then had been by long-wave transmissions only, and a U-boat had to surface and erect an aerial before being able to send or receive messages. This was a time consuming procedure even in the best of conditions, and in many circumstances it was just not practical, especially when under enemy threat, or when everything depended on a boat remaining unseen. For these reasons among others, attempts to plan transmissions at prearranged times failed. They could not take into account the changing events at sea; and denied a reliable wireless link, there was a limit to the opportunities which boats had of remaining within sight of each other and keeping contact by means of visual signalling.

Even in spite of these handicaps Doenitz, as a U-boat commander, had on occasion tried to act in company with another U-boat, setting off together and with a common plan. But he was not successful.

Now, in 1940, all that was changed. There was short-wave radio; U-boats could keep in touch with one another, and with the U-boat base, at most times. Doenitz at last had the means of organizing group attacks, and enough boats to carry them out.

At first he had visualized a surface warship or senior U-boat acting as 'command ship' to direct the U-boats into action. But he soon resolved that by far the best method was for all boats to keep closely in touch with base, and for himself to direct operations, leaving the business of the final assault to the individual commanders on the spot. This became a supremely practical solution after the fall of France, when the U-boat base was set up at Lorient.

The plan of attack by the 'wolf-pack' was simple. As a U-boat discovered a convoy it would report to base and continue to shadow the convoy while other boats in the area were directed to converge on the convoy and make the kill.

The second lesson which Doenitz had carried from the 1914-18 war was the value of a U-boat attacking at fast speed on the surface at night, when its small silhouette was extremely difficult to detect by lookouts. This surprise tactic had been carried out very successfully by some U-boat commanders, himself included, towards the end of that war.

So here was the double-edged master plan: U-boats attacking in groups, on the surface at night, and creating havoc.

There was, however, no question of Doenitz having kept these revolutionary tactics a deep, dark secret. As long ago as 1937, the German Navy had carried out its first large-scale manoeuvres in which U-boats tried out their group assaults, and this and subsequent exercises could hardly have escaped the notice of foreign naval intelligence. As for attacking by night, Doenitz had gone so far as to give warning to the world of his intentions. Just as Adolf Hitler had laid down his doctrine in 'Mein Kampf', so Doenitz also laid bare his thinking in a book. It was called 'Die U-bootwaffe' (The U-boat Force) and was published in Berlin in January, 1939 - just after the Munich crisis, and eight months before war began. In his book Doenitz stressed very strongly, by means of words *and* illustrations, the great advantages to be gained by U-boats attacking on the surface at night.

Yet apparently no one in Britain took the slightest bit of notice.

In the years up to 1939, while the German Navy had concentrated on perfecting its hydrophones, the Royal Navy had felt itself secure in the possession of the much superior asdic underwater detector. This, basically, emitted a high-frequency sound beam which 'pinged' on an undersea object and gave a highly accurate bearing. So although British naval training between the wars did include exercises with surfaced submarines, these were purely incidental, and the whole accent had been on submerged attack, and methods of defence against it. The plain truth was that the submarine was still regarded as an undersea craft and not, as Doenitz now saw it, a surface attacker taking on the role of a fast torpedo boat. As far as the Royal Navy was concerned, enemy submarines were expected to attack by day, submerged, and the asdic was the finest weapon British warships could wish for. As for U-boat action at night, they would be all right as the enemy would not be able to see them.

As it transpired, the efficiency of the asdic did take the Germans by surprise, but it was soon discovered that it only worked underwater and was virtually useless against a surfaced U-boat. And radar was not yet used at sea, being still, in its infancy, used mainly as a warning system to detect enemy aircraft over British skies.

The position, then, in October 1940 was that reports of surfaced U-boats, and of attacks by night, had been made by some British warships during the past month or two, but these had not been seen to indicate that any special new tactics were being employed by the enemy. Similarly, where definitely more than one U-boat had been spotted during an attack on a convoy, still no particular construction was placed on this. But in fact Doenitz's new style of U-boat warfare had already begun. During the early part of September he had organized, from Lorient, the first successful attack by a group of U-boats, which sank five ships of a convoy, while in late September a second group attack had achieved the staggering result of eleven ships sunk in a fifteen-ship convoy. Yet in spite of this calamitous loss the idea of deliberately organized attacks by groups of U-boats just did not percolate through to the Admiralty. Or at least if it did, certainly no warning of it was passed on to the escort commanders.

This was the situation when Admiral Doenitz planned his 'wolf-pack' strike against SC7. Now that Heinrich Bleichrodt's shadowing U-48 had been chased away from the convoy, all they knew at Lorient was the convoy's last position as Bleichrodt had reported it. What course would SC7 now take? It was impossible to judge with any certainty, for there was no way of knowing what evasive action the convoy might have taken. But there *was* another way of re-locating it. Doenitz now sent out new instructions to the five patrolling U-boats he had contacted earlier. This time they were ordered to withdraw to a point far ahead of the convoy's last known position and form up in line abreast, miles apart, in a vertical north-to-south line, or 'stripe'. Into this line, with a morsel of luck, SC7 would unwittingly sail. It was planned that the line of boats should be in position by daylight on October 18.

The five U-boats ordered to lay this ambush were commanded by some of the elite among Doenitz's carefully bred U-boat officers. Four of the commanders had been in the navy since 1930, and all were members of the pioneer nucleus with which he had begun to build the new U-boat arm in 1935, after Germany won the right to expand her navy under the Anglo-German Naval Agreement. Doenitz had taught them all he knew, and gone out with them in their boats during training They were now mature young men whose ages ranged from twenty-eight to thirty, and their experience and capabilities were of a very high order. All had graduated from smaller boats to their new big craft, which they had been sailing with success since early summer; and all had developed their talents in their individual ways, for Doenitz allowed his officers to evolve their own tactics in the light of practical experience. In this way, although the principle of night surface assault had not yet been written into the training textbooks, the 'aces' among them had already begun independently to use this method of attack.

So now the five commanders were to move their boats into action like a small fleet, hovering poised across the expected path of their prey. They were Fritz Frauenheim, in U-101; Karl-Heinz Moehle, in U-123; Engelbert Endrass, in U-46; Joachim Schepke, in U-100; and Otto Kretschmer, in U-99. Of them all, the two latter were perhaps among the best known U-boat commanders outside the service. Schepke, the tall and handsome twenty-eight year old with the ready smile, and Kretschmer, of the same age but with a serious look and demeanour.

Otto Kretschmer, the son of a teacher, was already well on his way to becoming Germany's greatest U-boat ace of World War II. 'Otto the Silent' was a disciplinarian, a cool, self-confident professional. He, more than any other, had been quick to see the advantages of surfaced attack by night, and in fact he had already abandoned completely the old practice of submerged attack on an escorted convoy by daylight, except when it was impossible for him to wait for darkness. His tactics now were to shadow by day and attack by night, moving into the convoy lanes and making every torpedo count, one to a ship, instead of standing off at a distance and firing what he considered to be wasteful 'fans' of three or four torpedoes across the path of the convoy, the method still employed in the classic submerged attack by daylight. These and other tactics Kretschmer had set out in his new Standing Orders for U-99, the craft with the familiar golden horseshoe emblem on its conning-tower, and they were the result of hard and highly successful practical experience.

He had already sunk the remarkable total of twenty ships by going in at them on the surface.

As the five U-boats travelled from various directions to take up their positions in the line of ambush east of Rockall, one other boat was busy patrolling in the reverse direction, heading westwards. This was U-38, commanded by Kapitanleutnant Heinrich Liebe. It was late in the evening of October 17, and Liebe could feel fairly satisfied with his day's work, for early that morning he had torpedoed and sunk by gunfire the Greek *Aenos*. Now he was searching for other game, and unexpectedly found it. Convoy SC7, sailing by right under his nose.

Near to midnight on the 17th, as the moon shone brightly, silhouetting the ships of the convoy to make them a dream of a target, he crept in close on the dark side to select his victims.

7

Don't Launch the Boats!

Friday, October 18. It was fifteen minutes past midnight, 0015 hours, when two more escorts sent to help bring in the convoy sighted SC7 ahead. The moon was behind cloud, but visibility was good, and the sea calm. All seemed quiet as the convoy forged on through the night. It had now reached position 58.50 N, 14.12 W, and would reach a point north of Rockall in less than six hours' steaming.

The two new arrivals, the sloop HMS *Leith* and corvette HMS *Heartsease*, were the last escorts allocated to the convoy. As they neared the columns of ships *Leith*, being the senior vessel, signalled the corvette to take up a flanking position while she herself took station astern. But just as they were positioning themselves the peaceful night scene changed.

U-38 had crept up unseen on the port side of the convoy, where only *Bluebell* was in station, the corvette's asdic being unable to detect the surfaced U-boat. *Fowey* was far away on the convoy's starboard side. As the masking clouds shifted from the face of the moon, Kapitanleutnant Liebe fired a salvo of torpedoes across the path of the convoy's silhouetted port column of ships. He was not very successful, scoring only one hit - on ship number thirteen of the convoy.

The Glasgow steamer *Carsbreck*, stacked high with timber, shuddered under the explosion and listed violently to port. As all hands rushed on deck the ship started to go down by the head. *Carsbreck* looked done for, some of her timber already on fire. Captain John Muir gave the order to launch the boats and abandon ship.

At the radios in other ships of the convoy they heard *Carsbreck*'s rapid distress call . . . 'SSSS' . . . repeated twice, followed by four or five attempts to tap out her call sign GYXB. The operator seemed unable to get it right, and his last attempt died off in the middle. They feared the worst.

On *Carsbreck* as the crew stood at their lifeboat stations a hurried roll call revealed that two young deck-boys were missing. The bosun and an A.B., together with the ship's cook, Hilton Brodie, ran down to the boys' accommodation, which was on the port side amidships, not more than forty feet from where the torpedo had struck. With difficulty they managed to open the door and found the two boys lying sound asleep, completely unaware of what was happening. The three men quickly roused the lads from their dreams and hurried them on deck.

The boats were being launched when Captain Muir, a Glasgow master in his sixties, suddenly reappeared on the boatdeck, very agitated.

'Don't launch them!' he cried. 'Don't launch the boats! It's all right, we are not sinking - come back, men - come back!'

As the captain's words were passed along from man to man they brought real confusion, for a change of order by the usually dour and very determined master was entirely unexpected and no one seemed to know how to cancel an order to abandon ship. But eventually the majority of the crew did come back, except for the men in one lifeboat which had pulled away from the ship.

The *Carsbreck* had taken a severe knock. The force of the explosion had swung her right round until she was now facing in the opposite direction to the fast disappearing convoy; she still listed badly to port and the foc'sle was almost under water, but, said her master and the chief engineer, she was not sinking and they were convinced she could still make passage. Once this was made clear the returned crew accepted the situation with relief. After all, they had withstood an attack without suffering a single casualty, which in itself was very heartening, and the ship was refusing to be beaten. Even the usually excitable Arab firemen had shown a praiseworthy coolness, and strangely no one seemed to fear the possibility of another torpedo.

Nor did it come. U-38 had used its superior surface speed to race ahead and position itself for another strike at the convoy.

Half an hour after *Carsbreck* was hit, Kapitanleutnant Liebe fired another salvo of torpedoes. This time, however, he was completely out of luck, none of them striking home. Commodore MacKinnon, looking out from the bridge of *Assyrian*, saw the track of one torpedo as it sped across the path of his ship and immediately signalled the convoy to make an emergency turn to starboard.

Fowey, miles away to starboard, made all speed to get round to the port side of the convoy and help *Bluebell* in her search for the U-boat, but the sloop's fourteen knots was far too inadequate and she did not meet up with *Bluebell* until thirty-five minutes after U-38's second salvo had been fired. The German, however, made no further attack during this time, and now the two escorts searched up the port side of the convoy, but without result. They were joined soon afterwards by the newcomers, *Leith* and *Heartsease*, and the search was repeated up and down the convoy's port side. But the U-boat had gone. Had it submerged they would have had a fair chance of detecting it, but the German had remained on the surface, using his fast diesel engines to elude his pursuers.

In fact, although they could not know it, U-38 would not renew its attack on SC7. After wirelessing the convoy's position to Lorient, Kapitanleutnant Liebe returned to his patrol.

In these eventful early hours of the morning of the 18th, *Leith*, being the senior of the escorts present, now assumed command. She took *Bluebell* in company, sent *Fowey* back to the convoy, and detached *Heartsease* to look for the torpedoed *Carsbreck*. But it was *Leith* herself who, after having abandoned her search for the attacker and turned to catch up with the convoy, first sighted *Carsbreck* and the lone lifeboat which had pulled away from the steamer. The time was 6.10 a.m.

In the early morning light the full extent of the damage to *Carsbreck* could now be seen. The torpedo had struck her just forward of amidships on the port side at No. 2 hatch; they were lucky to be loaded with timber, which gave the ship extra buoyancy, for there was a gaping hole in her side about thirty feet across, out of which planks of timber were escaping and littering the sea.

Leith drew close and her commander spoke to *Carsbreck*'s master by loudhailer. Was she in distress? How badly damaged was she?

Captain Muir replied that his crippled ship had a good chance of staying afloat and he should be able to keep her steaming at a steady six knots.

This was good news, but it also presented a problem. In the state she was in, *Carsbreck* could not be left to limp along alone. *Leith* therefore signalled *Heartsease* to remain behind and escort the damaged steamer after first picking up the men in the lifeboat and return them to their ship. *Leith* then, in company with *Bluebell*, set course for the convoy at fourteen knots, reaching it shortly after 9.30 a.m.

Leith now briefly exchanged signals with Commodore MacKinnon in *Assyrian*. The sloop was commanded by Commander Roland Charlton Allen, RN, a Dartmouth man and a very efficient officer, as well as a popular captain in the eyes of his largely Regular naval crew. After his rudely interrupted arrival on the scene - Allen had only just reached astern of the convoy when *Carsbreck* was struck - he was now to take a major role in the events to follow.

Leith, which he had commanded for about five months, was somewhat smaller than *Fowey*, being less than a thousand tons. She was also newer and a little faster, but her other refinements were few. She was fitted with the early type of asdic set where the operator sat on an open bridge, training the oscillator by means of a handwheel mounted on the binnacle. And she had only a magnetic compass, subject to all kinds of fluctuations, unlike the newer gyro kind. Her armament was similar to *Fowey*'s, a 4.7 in. gun on the foc'sle and a 3 in. gun on 'B' deck.

Like *Fowey*, the *Leith* had spent most of her time pre-war in warmer waters. Shortly before the war began she was on loan to the Royal New Zealand Navy, and paid an official visit to the Tonga Islands, embarking Queen Salote for a tour round her domain. Memories of the jolly queen's voyage were still vivid. Naturally she had been given the best accommodation the ship could provide, namely the captain's cabin. Salote being a very substantial lady, over six feet tall and about 18 stone in weight, the captain's bunk suffered as a result; her majesty broke its springs, and it was never the same again. After this diverting interlude *Leith* was all set to begin a pleasant six months tour of the South Sea Islands when she was abruptly recalled for war.

Her forty-year-old commander was an orderly, meticulous man known as 'Maudie' Allen to his intimates, after the noted dancer, but, good-humouredly, 'Auntie' Allen to others, because of his apparent zeal for working by the book. However, Commander Allen straightforward and courteous, was possessed of a knowhow that was often an inspiration to brother officers. For example, when able to leave the bridge at night he slept on his bunk with a faint blue light over it. When the officer of the watch saw anything he pressed a bell, and in two seconds Commander Allen was up, through the bathroom - also with a blue light and ever-open doors - and thence to the bridge. He could reckon on reaching the bridge in five seconds flat *and* with his eyes accustomed to the darkness. There were no flies on 'Auntie' Allen.

To the other SC7 escort commanders, however, he was a completely unknown quantity. He had not met any of them before, not Aubrey of *Fowey* nor Sherwood of *Bluebell*, nor even Lieutenant-Commander Edward John North, RNR, of *Heartsease*, the ship with which he had arrived. So the situation remained that all four escort commanders and their ships were complete strangers to each other, and they had no common plan against attack. It was now up to Allen, as the senior escort, to deploy them as he saw fit.

The late hours of the morning saw SC7 curving steadily to the south-east, north of Rockall. The gap in the port column had been closed, ship number fourteen, *Shekatika*, moving up to take the place of *Carsbreck* at number thirteen. Superstition apart, it was not a very comfortable move for her crew, after having seen the *Carsbreck* hit directly ahead of them and watched her reel back in the haze of moonlight and mist. But they were not alone in their thoughts. None of the merchant crews felt that trouble was past, especially with the sharp reminder given by the occasional glimpse of survivors moving about the decks of *Bluebell* and *Fowey*. At such times a man would get to wondering quietly which part of his ship would be hit if she did stop a torpedo . . . whether it would strike for'ard or aft or amidships. Would there be a gigantic flash, roar or blast? Or would he be transported from this life to the next without knowing how it had happened? It was a numbing kind of thought born of a peculiar mixture of fear, fatalism, and an almost detached curiosity.

They were now entering the zone of greatest danger, and with the convoy spread out over such a big area - there were still twenty-nine ships - it seemed that their few escorts faced an impossible task in trying to give protection to them all. Shortly after midday some ominous bits of wreckage were spotted floating in the sea, and there gradually came into view the pathetically waving occupants of two rafts, a sudden huddle of forlorn life tossing on the expanse of ocean. The survivors had roped their rafts together so they would not drift apart, and each was crowded, many of its occupants having to stand up, for the simple reason that there was not enough space for them all to sit or lie down at once.

Always wary of a trap, of a U-boat perhaps lying in wait near the scene for someone to take a 'bait', *Leith* and *Bluebell* searched the area around the rafts before the sloop finally closed in and took the survivors aboard. They were the master and eighteen members of the crew of the Estonian steamer *Nora?* They had been adrift for five days and nights, hanging grimly on to the rafts and praying for some ship to pass, since their vessel was torpedoed some fifty miles west of Rockall. They climbed aboard *Leith* weak and exhausted, but with their master still clutching two precious pieces of 'luggage': his sextant, and a briefcase containing the ship's papers.

It was a sombre rescue scene that caused nerves to be drawn a little tighter all round.

During the late afternoon Commodore MacKinnon began to run up signal flags. These gave early warning to all ships of his intention to alter the convoy's course by 40 degrees to starboard at 8 p.m., and then at 11.30 p.m., to swing the convoy back 40 degrees to port.

Commander Allen now formulated his plans for the escorts in the case of attack, and signalled them to *Fowey* and *Bluebell.* By day, he instructed them, *Leith* would pass through the convoy on a reciprocal course. The escort on the engaged side was to take station ahead, the escort on the other side to go astern, and then look out for the signal to turn 90 degrees. By night, the ship on the side not attacked was to take up station as directed and remain with the convoy. If the side of attack was unknown, both wing ships were to turn outward.

This understood, Allen now ordered *Fowey* to search five miles astern of the convoy at dusk, to shake off any shadowing U-boat, and then steam back to take up her position on the convoy's port side. Meanwhile *Bluebell* was to remain at her station on the starboard side.

Having delivered herself of these orders *Leith* steamed out in front of the convoy as *Scarborough* had done earlier in the voyage. *Heartsease* did not come into the scheme of things now, as she was far behind escorting the damaged *Carsbreck.*

The Glasgow ship, as good as her master's promise, was limping along at five or six knots, although every now and then there was a scare for her crew as she gave an extra heavy roll to port, when planks of timber would slip out through the huge hole in her side, leaving a plaintive trail across the ocean like in some weird paperchase.

It was an unusual role for *Heartsease*, playing nursemaid to a single damaged ship. The corvette was more used to being in the centre of any action, as on a recent convoy when she had run up her blue and yellow attack signal and depth-charged a U-boat. 'Heart Disease' her crew called her, for although a splendid seaboat she rolled frightfully and fairly rapidly. She was identical to *Bluebell*, having been launched during the same week, and like *Bluebell*'s commander, Lieutenant-Commander North had stood by his vessel as she was completed.

He was thirty-eight, and a man used to far bigger ships, having spent twenty years with the P. and O. Line; when war broke out he was chief officer of the liner *Strathaird*. But he had taken smaller ships in his stride and commanded anti-submarine trawlers before taking over *Heartsease*. A modest and unassuming Oxfordshire countryman with a big, hearty laugh, North was well liked by his officers and crew. He still managed to find humour in the fact that his stomach could never acclimatize itself to the small ships and that he was prone to seasickness when *Heartsease* left harbour, often sharing the same bucket on the bridge with his signalman. However, he bore the ship no malice, in fact he was well pleased with her. Pride of place in the wardroom was given to a little picture of wild heartsease growing on the fells above Tynemouth, which a friend had painted while on holiday.

In her short life *Heartsease* had already experienced some of the worst the Atlantic could offer. For half the time on her last trip out she had ridden a fierce gale during which she had lost her charges for nearly two days. The calmer weather now was altogether incongruous; was this really late October in one of the wildest of oceans?

The same thought was uppermost in the minds of many crews of the merchant ships in the convoy now drawn far ahead and out of sight. After a few days of turbulence the weather was once again proving far too kind; rough seas were infinitely preferable, for rough seas handicapped the enemy.

The daylight faded into darkness and at 8 p.m. as arranged, Commodore MacKinnon turned the convoy 40 degrees to starboard. The manoeuvre was carried out perfectly under the night sky and in a calm sea with a slight swell. The full moonlight had shone on them all as night descended, but now dark clouds veiled the face of the moon from time to time, and a fresh wind blew drifting patches of light mist.

The convoy settled down for the night. They could not know that in a matter of minutes it would begin to explode hellishly around them.

The five U-boats had formed their line of ambush well, helped by U-38's last reported position of SC7. The convoy had been sighted during the afternoon and the 'wolves' had waited for nightfall to pounce. They were uncertain about the strength of the escorts; the convoy had seemed from a distance to be guarded by at least three destroyers and several smaller warships, though this was certainly no deterrent. Each U-boat commander had his own plan of action. Some would fire 'fans' of torpedoes from outside the escort screen, or closer in as the action developed. The advantages of close-in surface attack would also be pressed. The boldest method was to be used by Otto Kretschmer in U-99, who intended to speed right inside the convoy lanes just as soon as he could dodge past the escorts.

This was the opportunity all had been waiting for. The big night.

At 8.15 p.m. Kapitanleutnant Engelbert Endrass in U-46 fired a first slavo of three torpedoes at the port bow of the convoy, which with *Fowey* still searching five miles astern was left completely unguarded. One torpedo found a target.

The destruction of convoy SC7 had begun.

8

The Night Explodes

The torpedo from U-46 ripped into the port side of the Swedish *Convallaria*, causing a huge explosion which shook the ship from stem to stern and shot parts of her deck cargo high into the air. She began to sink by the stern immediately. The order was quickly given to launch the two lifeboats, and in three minutes both boats were in the water with all hands, pulling hard away from the doomed vessel. Only five minutes later the 2,000-ton ship reared up vertically with her bow pointing to the sky, then slid back until only her foc'sle was above the surface of the water. She remained suspended like this for a full quarter of an hour, held uncannily afloat by her crammed cargo of pulpwood, then, with a sigh, she disappeared down into a thousand fathoms of the night black Atlantic.

Leith, steaming ahead of the convoy, had just reached the extreme starboard limit of her station when *Convellaria* was hit. She turned sharply and raced at full speed across to the port side, firing starshell to illuminate the scene as she went. She scoured the dark ocean for ten miles, but found no signs of the attacker and had to give up and turn back to the convoy.

Fowey, still making her asdic sweep astern of the convoy, saw the starshell fired by *Leith* and, in an attempt to find out what was happening tried to call up *Leith* on the convoy manoeuvring wave - a special W/T wavelength on which suitably equipped escorts could communicate with each other by morse transmission. There was no response, so *Fowey* hurried to regain her position up the port side, but she was an hour's steaming from the rear of the convoy and at her limited speed it was a long, frustrating haul back. On the way she sighted two lifeboats ahead. Although Admiralty orders were against escorts stopping to pick up survivors, Commander Aubrey now justified his decision to pick up the men in the boats on the grounds that they might be able to give him some useful information regarding the attack, as well as the fact that they were completely alone with no other ship standing by them - officialdom required more than simple humane reasons. The boats were found to contain the crew of the *Convallaria*, whose ship had long vanished. There was little delay in getting them aboard the sloop, but from an information point of view the Swedes were a complete write-off. All one officer could tell Aubrey when he was questioned on the bridge was 'There was a big bang, and I yumped for the yollyboat . . .'

Once more Aubrey tried to call up *Leith* on the convoy manoeuvring wave, but again there was no answer; either *Leith* did not possess the necessary equipment or it was not tuned in accurately. This was highly frustrating. After an eternity, as it seemed to *Fowey*'s commander, more used to the quick response of a fast destroyer than to the limited engines of his sloop, *Fowey* met up with *Leith* and joined her in a new search up the wake of the convoy, but there was still no trace of the enemy. In the meantime, as the convoy sailed on ahead with only *Bluebell* in station on its starboard bow, the wolves closed in.

The Cardiff steamer *Beautus*, laden with steel ingots and timber piled high, sighted a shadowy U-boat skimming the moonlit surface of the sea off her port bow. The radio officer tapped out the alarm, but moments later she rocked as a torpedo struck her between Nos. 2 and 4 holds. The sea rushed in and the big vessel, more than twice the size of *Convallaria*, shuddered to a stop and began to settle. After a quick inspection of the damage it was clear it would be only a matter of time before she sank. Captain Wilfred Brett gave the order to abandon ship.

There was confusion as one of the two lifeboats was being prepared for lowering by the native stokers; when told to knock out the toggle to release the griping brackets, they chopped through the hauling part of the falls, with the result that the boat crashed down into the sea and was so badly damaged as to make it unseaworthy. But *Beatus* carried a jollyboat and this was launched along with the other lifeboat. Eventually everyone had got away to the boats except Captain Brett and the ship's naval Reservist gunlayer, together with an Indian fireman. The fireman was a fatalist and refused to leave the ship. His time had come, he said, and he was content to stay and go down with the vessel. He was stubborn and unyielding, and the only way the captain and gunner could finally persuade him to go was by telling him that they had to be the last people to leave the ship and he *must* go before them. Grudgingly the fireman then consented to join one of the boats, though still voicing his protests. No sooner had he gone than the gunner, with rather excessive devotion to duty, insisted that *he* should be the last to leave, after first seeing the captain safely off. It was hardly the time for further argument, so to settle the matter they jumped together into the waiting boat.

The broken *Beatus* took forty minutes to die. While she was still inching below the surface the Dutch ship *Boekolo* came upon her two lifeboats of survivors and, surprisingly, slowed down and stopped engines with the evident intention of picking them up. This comradely gesture was against all instructions and unfortunately brought disastrous consequences. Only one seaman from *Beatus* had managed to climb up the Dutch ship's side before she, too, was hit by a torpedo and lurched crazily in the water, never to start her engines again.

They saw the whole thing happen from the bridge of *Bluebell* miles away, and could scarcely believe their eyes when the tramp from Amsterdam, the Dutch colours bold on her funnel, suddenly hove-to.

'Good God, what's that fellow stopped for?' exclaimed Commander Sherwood to one of his officers.

Next minute, the torpedo, and the third victim. Fire broke out among the timber cargo as *Boekolo*'s crew got away in their boats.

Aboard the big *Shekatika*, which was astern of *Beatus* when that ship reeled and fell away, Second Radio Officer Raymond Baldwin had picked up the urgent distress signals of all three ships. Now he was trying to keep up with events between rushing out through the double blackout curtains up to the bridge to give information to the captain in the gloom, the captain reading the messages over the binnacle light.

Baldwin had just returned to the radio cabin after his third or fourth run up to the bridge when there was a thunderous boom and an almost instant lurch of the ship as *Shekatika* became the wolf-pack's fourth victim.

His chair canted, but he managed to avoid being flung on to the floor. He stood up, thinking 'Surely that couldn't have been?' Although wearing earphones he could hear crashing noises of descending wood, and what sounded like torrents of rain. The radio cabin began to tilt over at an angle . . . ten, twenty degrees . . . There was a scurry of feet from the outer deck and First Radio Officer Harris appeared - 'This is it, we've been torpedoed!' Harris was carrying his life-jacket and now began to pull it on. Baldwin took his life-jacket down from the cabin bulkhead, put the blue kapok waistcoat on and tied its black tapes. . . .

The torpedo had struck *Shekatika* on the port side in the way of No. 4 hold, the explosion flinging up a mountain of pitprops aft by the mast where Nos. 3 and 4 holds joined. The noise of these pitprops hurtling back on to the deck and into the sea accompanied the torpedo explosion 'rain' which had been heard in the radio cabin - the ship's third mate narrowly missed being struck by one of the lethal lengths of flying wood.

The explosion, close to the men's quarters aft, had blown brass scuttles across cabins with terrific force, though fortunately hitting no one. The lights aft went out immediately. The descending waterspout roared down, making them think the stern was already awash, and men fled without pausing to snatch up belongings, scrambling in the dark over the great black pile of pitprops to amidships and the boats, bumping and bruising themselves and registering their curses as they went. By this time the ship's stern was already very well down.

Back in the radio room the heavy running of the captain was heard. 'Send th' SSSS, Sparrks!' Captain Robert Paterson's red face above the gold bands on his greatcoat shoulders vanished into the alleyway and the door of the safe in his day cabin clanged open as he seized the ship's accounts and stock of money. Harris began to send the SSSS message. Captain Paterson looked in again for a second, grasping a thick briefcase, then raced heavy footed back to the bridge.

Suddenly the listing ship seemed to right herself again. It came as a surprise, but the simple reason was that after bursting in on one side, the seawater had quickly run over the central propeller tunnel and flooded both halves of Nos. 3 and 4 holds, so that the water was evenly distributed. *Shekatika* was now kept afloat by her wood cargo.

In the moonlight the crew assembled on the boatdeck. The safety valve steampipe beside the funnel was fanning out steam in the steady earpaining hissing roar, for *Shekatika* had been thumping along at full speed when hit and great fires were fully stoked down below; the reciprocating engine was still, and steam roared skywards since the engine was not consuming it. On deck, conversation could only be carried on by shouting in each other's ears.

The captain again hurried to the radio room and it was decided to inform the shore that *Shekatika* had been hit. An international SOS message was now sent out and comfortingly answered by the coastal radio station at Valentia, in south-west Ireland.

Chief Officer Leask and Second Mate Alexander Smith went aft on deck to inspect the damage. The explosion had broken the tail-shift and buckled the bulkhead between No. 3 hold and the engine-room, making it impossible to close the watertight door to the shaft-tunnel, with the result that the sea was sluicing into the engine-room pretty fast.

The dynamo, with excess steam and now untended, was running high voltage, and the radio room was so brightly lit that the lamp threatened to burn out. It was time to quit. 'What about the log?' There was a considerable litter of papers and hours of writing up. 'Leave it, we'll just take the code books.' Baldwin drew out the emergency carborundum crystal that Board of Trade regulations insisted all ships must carry. Such a crystal allowed messages to be received without any electricity supply whatever. It went into his pocket as a souvenir as they pushed out into the dark with the weighted code bag.

Hunched on the boatdeck stood the Scottish chief engineer. Into his hand Baldwin slipped a borrowed pack of patience cards which he had grabbed from his cabin along with his coat. 'Don't say I lost them, Chief!' he bellowed. The chief looked at him as if he were mad, but thrust the cards silently into his pocket.

Far below, the second engineer was at that moment studying the seawater pouring into the flooded engine-room through the buckled watertight door to the tunnel. When he admitted a little steam to the triple expansion engine it thundered round and the whole ship shook, for its great crankshaft had no load to carry. The main propeller shaft was broken and the ship helpless, but the captain had insisted that this should be made doubly sure of before they abandoned ship. The engineer on watch had previously shut down the flailing engine before fleeing aloft.

Looking aft, the once orderly stacks of pitprops were now a tangled mountain, while hundreds more props dipped and bobbed black on the surface of the sea under the cold light of the moon. The ship swayed with a new dead motion, her decks treacherously wet from the cascade of water that had followed the torpedo blast. Captain Paterson, an Edinburgh master in his late thirties, now had to make his decision. . . .

At this moment the searching *Fowey* sighted the dark, drifting shape of *Shekatika* from half a mile away. Her signal lamp blinked.

The sloop's morse message was read by half a dozen pairs of eyes on *Shekatika* and acknowledged by the chief officer with a brief flash of his hand torch at the end of every word.

'Are you in distress?' asked *Fowey*.

They grimaced their wry amusement. The fierce roar of steam made several rich comments inaudible.

'Yes,' flashed the torch.

'Are you abandoning ship?'

Captain Paterson looked around at the dark clusters of men, more than two dozen of them, awaiting his next word. Sadly, reluctantly, he nodded to the chief officer - 'Aye.'

'Yes,' flashed the torch again.

They clambered into the boats in an orderly manner, and in the general air of politeness there was almost strong competition to remain on board to pay out the ropes. The boats jerked down the big ship's sides into the shadow, and when the sea slapped them, their occupants found themselves swirling up and down about eight feet on the agitated water. The falls were unhooked at the ends of each boat and the men who had paid out the ropes came sliding down. Shouts of 'Mind the blocks!' could be faintly heard above the still searing noise of the steam. Oars were unshipped and they crabbed away from the great moonlit hulk, pulling their way gingerly through menacing pitprops that continually bumped the boats. Once round the bow of the ship they could see for the last time the name *Shekatika*, grey painted over though it was. The men, some clad only in thin singlets, hunched together.

Captain Paterson was in charge of one boat, Chief Officer Leask taking the other, as they hauled across to *Fowey* in the moderate swell. Only when boarding the sloop did the company suffer their first casualties. It was a tricky business having to jump from boat to ship on the crest of the waves. The captain fractured his right foot when it was caught between the lifeboat and *Fowey*'s side, and a seaman fell and injured his ribs.

Fowey's engine-room telegraph clanged, and the empty lifeboats drifted quickly astern into the night. On the messdecks the men from *Shekatika* began to loosen their life-jackets and fling them down at their feet.

'Hey - don't do that!' exclaimed some of the survivors already on board. 'They say this tin can would only last about ten seconds if she got a torpedo.'

When *Fowey* drew away from *Shekatika* the big Scots steamer was still well afloat on her packing of wood. Steaming hard after the convoy now, *Fowey* had not gone far before she sighted two more lifeboats, and once again the desperate question of whether to stop and take on survivors or continue on to try to regain the convoy confronted Commander Aubrey. But he did not hesitate. *Fowey* closed the boats and took aboard the crew of *Boekolo*, together with the one seaman from *Beautus* who had managed to board the Dutch ship before she was hit. Then on again after the convoy, by now drawn many miles ahead.

But the wolves were striking again, and with terrible result. The old British steamer *Creekirk*, which had won safely through one war, now stood no chance at all when a torpedo tore a gaping hole in her side. The 4,000-ton vessel was loaded with iron ore and she started to sink at once. What drama was played out in the last quick minutes of her long life no one survived to tell. From Guernsey-born Captain Elie Robilliard to the sixteen-year-old cabin boy, all thirty-four of her crew were killed or drowned along with her as she plunged to the bottom without trace except for a few pitiful bits of wreckage.

Aboard the big ex-American *Empire Miniver*, leading ship of a column on the starboard side of *Assyrian*, they had watched explosion follow explosion and the sky light up with gunflashes, starshell and parachute flares. The protecting darkness when the moon clouded over had gone, and all felt very naked and exposed.

In the midst of it all the bosun, a big burly man with a woollen comfort on his head, climbed the bridge ladder to see the master. Captain Robert Smith, a North Shields master who was no stranger to action at sea, had ordered the crew to keep awake and fully dressed, every man wearing his life-jacket, and now the bosun asked if some of the men could stand-easy, as those due to take the middle-watch, midnight to 4 a.m., wanted to turn in and get some sleep. But Captain Smith told him that in the present dangerous situation it was more important than ever that every man should stay fully dressed and out of his bunk, and the master promptly gave a further shrewd order to ensure it. He instructed the chief steward that every man off-watch was to be given a large tot of rum, but that he must come amidships to drink it. The order worked.

Now, after having seen several ships torpedoed, two of them very close to *Empire Miniver*, Captain Smith was turning over the idea of trying to make a run for it, away from what appeared to be certain destruction. *Empire Miniver* being an oil-burner and turbine driven, her speed had been kept down a little to conform to that of the convoy. The master knew that if he left the convoy he would be breaking regulations, but that was really a secondary consideration now; if he could get away from the area at full speed he might have a chance of saving his ship and his men. He finally reached a decision and ordered Third Mate Gilbert Hing to ask the chief engineer to let him have all the speed of which the vessel was capable.

Hing made his way down to the deck, hurried along the port alleyway to the chief's cabin and passed on the captain's request, at which Chief Engineer Paul, from Glasgow, a quiet and likeable man, disappeared into the engine-room to begin the great race.

Farther on down the passageway Hing came upon Third Engineer Sneddon, wearing only a towel round his waist and nothing else but his slippers. Calmly, Sneddon said he was going to have a bath. Hing reminded him of the captain's 'all fully dressed' order, but it didn't make a scrap of difference, the engineer was determined to take his plunge.

Up on the bridge they saw *Assyrian*'s gun firing, and other ships seemed to be firing too. Some of the shells were coming dangerously close. After that everything seemed to happen very quickly.

The torpedo that found *Empire Miniver* should by rights never have reached her. It was heading straight for the old steamer *Clintonia*, less than half the size of the ex-American, but *Clintonia*'s Captain Thomas Irvin skilfully swung his ship away from its path and the torpedo ran across to the bigger vessel. Even in the tension of that moment Captain Irvin hoped that Captain Smith would forgive him for dodging the torpedo; they had both begun their careers with the Stag Line and knew each other well.

Chief Officer John Green had just come up on to *Empire Miniver*'s bridge and was standing in the port wing looking over the ship's side when he saw the track of the torpedo speeding towards them. 'Mind your hat!' he yelled. Seconds later the torpedo struck. It tore into *Empire Miniver* amidships on the port side between the engine-room and the tank where the fuel oil was carried, blowing part of the port side away and shattering the port lifeboats above, even though they were American boats made of steel. Pigs of iron in the No. 3 'tweendecks shot up into the air over the funnel and rained down on the poop, where the frightened gun-crew jumped overboard after releasing a raft into a sea already afire with burning oil. The ship's engines stopped dead, plunging everything into pitch darkness, steam hissing up from below where Chief Engineer Paul lay dead, killed instantly in the explosion along with the fourth engineer and a fireman.

The ship, heavily laden with iron and steel, rapidly lost way and began to settle. Her welldecks were quickly awash and all hatchboards on the hatch abaft the bridge had been blown away, leaving a gaping hatchway. She could break her back and sink very quickly. Captain Smith gave instructions to abandon, shouting his order from the bridge to hands on deck below.

Chief Officer Green rang down 'Stop' on the engine-room telegraph, an unnecessary action with all contact with the engine-room destroyed, but one that came automatically. Third Mate Hing, as officer of the watch, lit and hoisted the red lights which told other ships they had been torpedoed. Hurrying down to the lower bridge Hing then saw Captain Smith trying to open the door leading to his quarters, and lent him a hand. But despite their combined efforts the door remained jammed fast.

On deck, Hing and Second Mate Reginald Leach tried to release the starboard liferaft from its securing pins, but it would not run, so they made their way aft and climbed the ladder to the boatdeck. An engine-room grating had been blown away and they had to be careful moving round the exposed opening in the half light of the moon. Then Chief Officer Green suddenly spotted Captain Smith crossing the boatdeck. 'Leap, Cap!' he yelled. The master reacted instantly, only realising afterwards that had he not done so he would have fallen down the entire depth of the ship.

While all were busy launching the starboard lifeboats an apparition appeared flying across the boatdeck in the shape of Third Engineer Sneddon, clad only in his jockey underpants. In the explosion he had been spreadeagled on the floor of the engineers' bathroom, half covered with small octagonal tiles, looking dazedly up through the torn ship at the clouds and stars above. Another latecomer was a greaser, the only survivor of the explosion in the engine-room. When the torpedo struck he had been at his duties in the after end of the propeller tunnel and, escaping unhurt, had managed to feel his way through the ship in total darkness and climb up the Jacob's ladder to the deck.

Steam was escaping from pipes on the boatdeck and the glands of the ship's siren as the two lifeboats got away, the captain in charge of one and the second officer taking the other. It was only ten minutes since the torpedo had struck, and yet it seemed a lifetime. One boat picked up all but one of the gun-crew from their raft. The missing man, the young ship's carpenter, was believed lost. But an hour later much shouting was heard from a floating light in the water and they found the carpenter, who had jumped overboard, still swimming for all he was worth and pushing the light in front of him.

The two boats kept within hailing distance as their occupants gazed out at the dismal night scene around them. Small lights from other lifeboats and liferafts could be seen twinkling on the surface of the sea. They could also see a few ships, stragglers possibly, at the tail end of the convoy. Even from their own 'dead stop' position these vessels seemed to be moving painfully slowly. . . .

The Cardiff steamer *Fiscus* had pushed on at a punishing ten knots, laden as she was with her cargo of steel. For Captain Ebenezer Williams, who had lived with the morbid presentiment of disaster long before the convoy sailed, this night's pattern of destruction had already exceeded even his worst fears. More than anyone he must have watched in horror the slaughter around him. But what it felt like to see a premonition unfold in reality before one's eyes he would never be able to tell, for the torpedo that now struck *Fiscus* caused one of the most violent explosions of the night, the ship almost disintegrating under the master's feet. She plunged like a stone, taking every one of her crew with her. Twenty-eight souls, from the forty-eight-year-old master to the two youngest members of his crew, brothers aged fourteen and fifteen, the sons of a widowed mother back in Cardiff.

The almost unbelievable tragedy was witnessed by those aboard the steamer *Somersby*. One minute *Fiscus* was steaming hard, the next she had erupted and vanished from the surface of the sea as if sucked down by some evil whirlpool.

Far away to the rear of the convoy another explosion followed, but this time the torpedo rocked an empty, derelict ship . . . the *Shekatika*. A different U-boat from the one that had first attacked her had now found the silently drifting vessel and given her the *coup de grâce*. The German withdrew, marking a 'kill', but when he had gone, still the battered *Shekatika* remained astonishingly afloat. . . .

Aboard the *Gunborg* earlier they had seen their fellow Swede, *Convallaria*, torpedoed and felt helpless when they could not stop to pick up survivors. But now they too, fell a victim of the pack.

A torpedo struck *Gunborg* on the port side, causing such a wild explosion that an enormous sea was thrown up over the vessel and her master was twice knocked down by a wall of hurtling water. The ship began to list heavily to port. Everyone ran for the lifeboats, including the youngest able seaman, Sture Mattsson, now torpedoed for the second time in weeks - he had lost his ship coming out, and here was his return ship shuddering and dying beneath him. On reaching the boatdeck Mattsson was suddenly aware of the strangeness of the moonlit scene, which was being enacted in complete silence, not a word coming from anyone as they got the lifeboats away as coolly and efficiently as if it was the kind of thing they did every day.

When the lifeboats had pulled away from *Gunborg* Mattsson remembered with a pang that in the rush he had left his dog on board. It was a fine dog, his German Shepherd, and, left shut up in his cabin, the animal was doomed to a horrible death as it went down with the ship. Mattsson told the master, Captain Jiewert, about the unfortunate animal. The captain studied the sinking ship. *Gunborg* was settling very slowly, kept afloat by her pulp-wood cargo; he decided there was time to go back. As the lifeboat pulled close to the vessel's side, Mattsson jumped on board and ran to his small cabin, opened the door and let the dog out, raced back on deck with it and threw it into the lifeboat, though the animal was frightened and he thought it might bite him. Minutes later they had pulled away from *Gunborg* again and were watching her slowly settle into the black sea, the grim-faced men and the boy, now happy at having saved his dog.

When the sea closed above *Gunborg* they began to row, seeing ships burning around them. Then a big vessel loomed up out of the darkness, silhouetted by the moon. She was the old Greek *Niritos?*

'Stand by to come aboard!' came an unexpected shout from the Greek as she slowed down to help them.

The surprised Swedes quickly talked it over among themselves and decided to refuse the offer. The truth was they all felt much safer in the lifeboats while the attack on the convoy continued.

They shouted their thanks across to the Greeks and told them of their decision.

'We wish you the best of luck!' came the reply from *Niritos*, and the big steamer made speed and passed on into the night. Hardly ten minutes later the lifeboats from *Gunborg* shuddered under the shock wave as the Greek vessel was hit by a torpedo. They could see the old sulphur-laden tramp across the sea in the moonlight, reeling from the explosion in a great cloud of dust and smoke. She sank very quickly, burning fiercely as she went. In Mattsson's boat no one spoke; silently their eyes followed the luckless Greek until she had gone, leaving only a wreath of smoking wreckage. They started to row again and, seeing a light on the water, pulled towards it to investigate. It was a lifeboat with a small lamp at the bow, its only occupant a dead seaman. They rowed on . . .

Across the sea strewn with shadowy wreckage, tossing and swirling, a single boatload of survivors from *Niritos* also pulled on their oars, though it seemed useless for them to head in any direction at all except away from drifting dangers. There were only fourteen of them, including the captain. More than half the crew had been killed in the explosion or drowned, or perhaps even now were struggling in the water somewhere in the dark. They would not survive.

It was now just after 10.30 p.m. In two explosive hours nine ships had been lost, though in the mass of distress signals received and half received by *Assyrian*'s radio officer there was no clear count. Commodore MacKinnon had seen his convoy all but shattered. The remaining twenty ships were now steaming as fast ahead as they could go, the majority of them still clinging to a desperate formation.

It had all been like a nightmarishly unreal picture of events played out against a theatre screen. Everything in darkness except for the light of the moon as it broke through mist and cloud, and against this backdrop the sudden flashes and explosions, the fires aboard stricken ships, the bobbing lights of lifeboats and rafts, strange flares streaking the sky, and eerily bursting starshell. Through all this the unharmed ships had moved darkly over the water, fleeing from the revealing moonlight and the unseen enemy, sometimes the frenzied note of a ship's siren sounding as vessels narrowly escaped collision in the scramble to avoid torpedoes seen streaking across the sea. As they steamed on, every cloud that momentarily obscured the face of the moon seemed to spell the difference between life and death.

For the ever searching escorts, never able to rejoin the convoy, the prolonged slaughter was both appalling and mystifying. How could one U-boat, or even two, manoeuvre to make these persistent attacks? Why could the enemy not be detected? The effect on the asdic hydrophones from the engines of the scattered merchant ships, the noises of torpedoes exploding, the echoes from debris and half sunken wrecks, made conditions extremely difficult, but why was not one contact made with an enemy boat? The unexplained flares, ships on fire, explosions first from one direction and then another, gave them a feeling of impotence. Like a blind man in a boxing ring they were being hit but did not know from which direction.

Then at last something tangible and real offered itself in the confusion of the night. At 10.40 p.m. the searching *Leith* sighted a U-boat on the surface dead ahead, racing fast on the same course as the sloop at a distance of about two miles. *Leith* fired more ten-second bursts of starshell as she gave chase. The U-boat and its wake were clearly visible, but not sufficiently for the sloop's 4.7 in. gun to get its sights on the German before he submerged minutes later. Continuing hot in pursuit *Leith* gained an asdic contact at less than two miles and held it on a run-in up to 800 yards - but then lost it.

It was a bitter disappointment. Either the U-boat had changed course at a speed far greater than that believed possible, or else the contact had been made on the boat's wake and not on the boat itself.

Aboard *Fowey* there had been some sharp criticism of *Leith*'s constant firing of starshell. It seemed totally unnecessary on such a night, showing nothing more in the moonlight than they could already see, and it was a giveaway to the enemy, quite apart from its natural handicap of the brilliant flash of the discharge temporarily blinding the ship's own lookouts. But perhaps *Leith* had orders which they did not have to take this course of action?

Bluebell, which had dropped back to help *Leith*, was now ordered to join in the hunt for the U-boat, which went on for another hour. But it was no use, the German had got clean away. Ordering *Bluebell* to stand by and pick up survivors of a number of torpedoed ships *Leith* swept off after the convoy, which had pulled far ahead and out of sight.

For *Bluebell*, moving into the scene of incredible devastation, a sea covered with wreckage, there began the long task of rounding up everyone alive in the water. It was near to midnight when the corvette started her mercy work. After tracking down survivors in their boats she searched the vicinity thoroughly for a lurking enemy before closing in and bringing the men aboard, a laborious operation in the rising wind and swell. The rescued men were the Swedes from the *Gunborg*, their captain very irate at being torpedoed although a neutral, the two boatloads from *Empire Miniver*, and the lucky ones from *Niritos*. The Greeks, some of them injured but none seriously, took an interminable time getting aboard. For Commander Sherwood, who had looked on wonderingly at the dog brought aboard by the Swedes, it was too much.

'Someone,' he said, 'must be looking for his bloody parrot!'

Bluebell, already carrying seventy survivors before beginning this latest rescue work, was feeling the strain on her limited resources.

'Bring aboard any blankets or food,' the men in the lifeboats were ordered. 'Any clothes - anything useful you've got. And hurry!' Every minute the corvette was stopped increased the danger.

Empire Miniver's Third Mate Hing, having been responsible for his ship's boats, knew where everything was stowed in them and it took only a few moments to pass over blankets, tinned meat, and a bottle of brandy from his boat; unfortunately the captain's boat drifted away with its brandy. In normal practice the plugs would have been taken out of the lifeboats so that they would sink and not litter the sea, but on this occasion the boats were left intact. . . they might yet save the lives of any man swimming in the water.

It was 3.15 a.m. before *Bluebell* could wireless Western Approaches Command: 'Have on board captain and crew of British ship *Empire Miniver* . . . Captain and 22 crew Swedish steamer *Gunsborg* . . . Captain and 13 crew Greek steamer *Niritos* . . . Standing by for further survivors at daylight.'

Bluebell, the ship whose raw company had never in their lives even seen a U-boat, now carried more than 140 survivors, but her job was by no means finished yet.

On leaving *Bluebell* at midnight, *Leith* had hurried off at her best speed to catch the convoy. After ten minutes she sighted *Fowey* and they talked by signal lamp. *Fowey* was now crammed with more than 150 survivors - the crews of *Convallaria*, *Shekatika* and *Boekolo*, besides the men rescued from the ship lost on the outward-bound convoy.

Leith stationed *Fowey* a mile on her port beam and together they raced after the convoy at *Fowey*'s top speed of 14 knots. At half-past midnight, great flashes lit up the sky on the starboard horizon and the two sloops altered course towards them. But they were hopelessly too late. The unguarded convoy had already been set upon by the wolf-pack in a staggering new wave of destruction.

9

And Still the Slaughter

At almost the same time as *Leith*, searching miles from the convoy sighted a surfaced U-boat, so did *Assyrian*, still leading the depleted convoy as the first ship of the centre column.

'Look, there goes Jerry!'

Captain Reg Kearon sent down from the bridge for Second Engineer William Venables, who hurried up to find the captain and Commodore pointing excitedly over the ship's bows.

'There's a U-boat ahead,' said the captain. 'Give us all the speed you've got, Sec, we're going to try and ram him!'

Venables shot a glance for'ard before making a run for the engine-room. On the moonlit sea barely a hundred yards ahead he could see the dark conning-tower of a U-boat.

Down in the stokehold the duty firemen, two young Liverpool lads and a first-trip trimmer, had been working steadily to keep the ship going at a good seven knots. Their faces lit up when Venables told them of the captain's plan, and that he was going to open the expansions to suck up every pound of steam they could produce. Grinning at the thought of the old ship ramming a U-boat they set to work like the very devil and fired her boilers as they had never been fired before; even with both engines full out her steam was on the feather.

From the bridge, Commodore MacKinnon signalled other ships of his intention to engage the U-boat on the surface and ordered every vessel to fire at the enemy on sight. Then *Assyrian* began to pull ahead of the convoy.

In the engine-room as the steam pressure rose, Venables opened up the expansions of the ship's twin steam-reciprocating engines to increase the revs. *Assyrian*'s normal speed was 104 r.p.m., but now the revs were 110, the fastest those engines had ever turned. Never before had the old vessel vibrated with such power. For the first time in her life she actually made ten knots,

For forty minutes she remained so hot on the U-boat's tail that it dared not try to turn away from her, so exposing itself to her after gun. But *Assyrian*'s best was not enough. As dark clouds momentarily obscured the moon, the U-boat seized the opportunity to veer away to starboard.

For a fraction of time *Assyrian*'s gun-crew on the four-inch were given a clear sight of the German. They fired twice, but missed. In the poor light the U-boat either submerged or disappeared at a fast speed into the night.

Second Mate Frank Bellas, the ship's gunnery officer, cursed the fact that they had no for'ard gun, when they might have got in a perfect shot while on the German's tail. But guns in the forepart of merchant ships were banned by International Regulations.

Engineer Venables, who had raced back on deck to see the action, now went below to reduce speed to normal to save overheating the ship's engines. The Commodore ordered the gunners to set off some smoke-floats. At first these flamed, making the ship an ideal target, then a dense pall of smoke trailed from her stern. It was just as if an old hen had spread her wings to protect her chicks.

Gradually *Assyrian* dropped back to resume her position at the head of the convoy.

Two other ships close to her had glimpsed the U-boat. The Dutch *Soesterberg* fired once, but then lost the German before the gun could be loaded with a new shell. The *Empire Brigade* also saw the surfaced U-boat only 200 yards ahead, surging along incongruously almost as if it were part of the convoy. But no action could be taken other than to alert the other ships: 'U-boat ahead on surface DE 53 . . .'

On the *Soesterberg* now all hands on deck except those on-watch stood by the lifeboats wearing their life-jackets. The chief officer paced the lower bridge, having made sure everything on the boatdeck was in order to lower the boats, while the gun-crew stood ready at their stations. The constant sharp lookout played tricks. Several times the bridge telephone rang as the gun-crew, thinking they could see a U-boat, asked permission to shoot. But Captain de Jong and his officers had good binoculars and could see nothing in the fluctuating darkness. He told the gunners not to shoot before he gave the order, as he was worried they might fire mistakenly at another merchant ship.

Assyrian's gunners were just as tense. After the nervous excitement of chasing the U-boat there had come the sobering thought that the Commodore ship, by her audacious attack, had probably singled herself out as a special target for the enemy. Tension mounted as she narrowly missed being hit by two torpedoes which skimmed past her stern. Two more barely missed her bow.

On the bridge, Chief Steward James Daley asked the captain if he should send up some tea. Captain Kearon told him to ask the Commodore, who was on the starboard side peering hard out into the night. Daley went across to him.

'Would you like me to send up some tea, sir?'

Commodore MacKinnon did not turn, or raise his voice. 'An excellent idea,' he said quietly, 'so long as it is for everybody.'

It was a reply Daley would think about many times afterwards, always with admiration, that in spite of the danger of the moment the Commodore could still remember his staff.

Daley left the bridge and went below to the pantry. He was completely unaided now, as the assistant stewards formed part of the gun-crew. But on the way down he met Engineer Venables, who was off-watch and quickly volunteered his help. Between them they made the tea, and Venables went aft to the gun-crew carrying a large well-filled jug and a pint mug.

But they never got their tea on the bridge.

The time was twenty minutes past midnight, although down in the engine-room, clocks and watches gave the time as almost midnight, for in the stress of convoy battle the usual practice of advancing the engine-room clock to compensate for west to east progression had been neglected. This discrepancy in time grimly affected the fate of the three firemen in the stokehold, who should have been relieved and on deck, and of their three mates now about to descend the 'fiddley' ladders to take over the watch.

Just before midnight by the engine-room's unaltered clock, Bill Venables, after taking up the tea to the gun-crew, looked into the stokehold to congratulate the two young firemen and the trimmer on their efforts in speeding the ship after the U-boat. He then went on deck to warn the oncoming midnight to 4 a.m. watch against making too much smoke. The watch, two firemen and a trimmer, had already gone to the fiddley, just forward of the funnel, and begun to descend the series of iron-runged ladders and gratings taking them down to the stokehold forty feet below, a hazardous job under blackout conditions. Venables ran along the port side of the ship to catch them up. As he did so there was a violent crash and explosion as a torpedo tore into *Assyrian*'s starboard side just forward of the engine-room, flinging Venables heavily to the deck and knocking him unconscious.

One minute after the torpedo hit Assyrian *another torpedo ripped into the* Empire Brigade. Soesterberg *was close by both ships. Captain de Jong immediately gave the order 'Hard-a-port!', trying to turn* Soesterberg *180 degrees and steam away from the U-boat. But barely was the Dutch ship turned four degrees when she, too, was hit.*

Five men died in the shattering explosion in *Assyrian*'s stokehold. On deck, three luckless off-watch firemen also caught the blast. They were standing in their life-jackets on the boatdeck beside the starboard lifeboat when the sudden fierce eruption hurled them overboard into the sea. The bow of the starboard lifeboat was smashed and the boat hung over the side swinging uselessly from a single bent davit. A long steel hatch-beam burst up through the hatchboards and tarpaulins of No. 3 hold and stood poised like a finger of warning. The engines stopped on impact, all lights went out and everywhere there was a loud hissing of steam.

Not realizing that he must have lain unconscious in the scuppers for several minutes, Bill Venables scrambled to his feet and ran along the deck to the engine-room entrance. A vestige of moonlight crept through a shattered skylight and found evil gleams in the black and oily water which surged sluggishly over the submerged engines. The smell of steam was overpowering, though by some strange quirk of the explosion not a steampipe was fractured.

With little hope for the safety of the fourth engineer, who had been on watch, Venables started down the engine-room ladder calling his name. There was no answer. With a louder shout he took another step down the ladder, slipped and plunged into the black water. In a panic he threshed about in the darkness until he regained the sanctuary of the ladder, to which the clung gasping for breath. It was only as he wiped the oily water from his eyes that he realised that his glasses had been lost and his forehead was bleeding from the fall on deck.

He staggered to his cabin for spare glasses and a torch, and again searched the water in the flooded engine-room. But there was no sign of the fourth engineer or any survivor. Heartsick, he hurried to the boatdeck.

But in fact Fourth Engineer William Dean had had a remarkable escape. The tremendous explosion had thrown him hard on to the stopped port engine, yet shocked and bruised as he was, he managed to climb up the ladder topside in the darkness and make his way to the ship's port side. Here, in the moonlight, under the supervision of the captain, men had been swarming down ropes and ladders into the port lifeboat. Dean climbed down after them and the boat began to drift away almost immediately.

Steward Jim Daley, caught in the crash and the dark as he was about to take the tea up to the bridge, felt his way out of the pitch darkness of the pantry and up the ladder to the boatdeck. By now the well-laden port boat was away from the side of the ship but already in difficulties. It had been holed, and quickly let in the sea until it was floating below the waterline on its tanks. There being no part of the boat visible, it seemed to those on the ship gazing after it that its passengers were all standing in the sea, when in fact they were sitting on the submerged gunwales. Among them was Engineer Dean, still badly shaken from his ordeal in the engine-room. A greaser beside him sat on Dean's left leg to prevent it from dithering, not with cold, although all he had on was his boiler-suit and socks, but with shock.

Captain Kearon called from the boatdeck to Third Mate Robinson, who had charge of the precariously floating boat, to row or paddle it farther away from the ship in case *Assyrian* suddenly plunged. Meanwhile the ship's young third engineer had swung out Tarzan-like across the water on a derrick line in an attempt to reach the lifeboat. He succeeded in getting there, but on seeing that the boat was almost sinking held tight to the rope and had to be pulled back to safety aboard the ship.

Everyone left on board now hurried to launch the small rafts which the ship carried in her rigging . . .

Across the water in the mist, moonlight and dark, *Soesterberg* reeled drunkenly. The torpedo had struck her at the rear of the engine-room, the explosion sending a huge column of water cascading over the vessel. The engine-room watertight doors, kept closed as much as possible against emergencies, burst open with the enormous air pressure, the starboard lifeboat disappeared with its davits and all into the sea, and four of the crew were sucked up by the enormous waterspout and hurled overboard.

On the bridge, as all the ship's lights went out, the engine-room telegraph was rung to 'Stop', though the engine had already stopped itself. Everything in sight of the bridge was a dark mess of twisted and burst metal and scattered pitprops. Captain de Jong ordered 'All men abandon ship in the port lifeboat.'

The ship was listing over, but the boat, like the one that had been blown away, was already swung out over the water and only needed to be lowered. The captain now wanted to give orders to his third and fourth mates, but in the general scramble both officers had already run off to the boatdeck with the seamen, while the gun-crew aft had taken a small raft, thrown it over the side and jumped after it; they were now clinging to it in the sea.

The master hurried to his cabin, grabbed the bag with the ship's secret papers and ran to the boatdeck. Everyone was sitting ready in the lifeboat, the chief officer at the rudder. The master grabbed an axe and started to cut the boat's lashings free. He called for help, and eventually the third mate scrambled back from the boat to lend him a hand. Together they freed the boat and paid it down to the water.

Second Mate Ort, who had been on radio duty, now appeared and tried with the help of a seaman to get the ship's remaining small boat into the water, but there was a knot in the tackle and the boat stuck fast halfway down the ship's side. The seaman gave up, jumped out of the boat into the sea and swam to the lifeboat.

The boat was anxious to go, but the master checked and found that the duty engineers were missing. He ordered the boat to wait while he and the second mate, armed with a torch, went to the black bowels of the ship in search of them. The steps in the engine-room had disappeared and the inrushing water was already some seven feet high, covered with a swirling mass of pitprops. There was no answer to their repeated shouts, and as they could not get down any lower they abandoned the search; all on duty must have died in the explosion. They returned to the lifeboat.

Soesterberg had now settled deeper in the water and the lifeboat was bucking and tossing just off her side. 'You jump first, Ort,' ordered the master, a small man but large in courage. The second mate refused, insisting that he would see his captain safely off first. In the end they jumped together, the master falling into the pitching lifeboat with nothing more than a bruise, but the mate, afraid of being trapped between the ship and the boat, jumping into the sea beyond the boat. The boat's line was cut and Ort was pulled aboard in seconds. To the captain's astonishment the boat was half full of water, and the level was rising. It must have been pierced by a lump of iron flung out in the engine-room explosion, yet no one was doing a thing about it.

'Bale!' ordered the captain. 'Bale as hard as you can, or we'll all drown!'

But those men who were not rowing simply sat there dull-eyed with shock. No one moved. 'I'm wounded,' one seaman weakly excused himself.

Angrily Captain de Jong grabbed a bucket and started quickly baling out, at the same time keeping an eye on the oarsmen to see that they pulled in the right direction to pick up the four gunners from the raft. Second Mate Ort, his only staunch helper, groped in the dark water in the boat searching for the leak. He found it, a big hole in the bottom.

'Take off your boots and shoes and bale out!' the captain ordered everyone. 'And give me your socks - quickly!'

This time they did as they were told. The master collected the socks and stuffed them together to make a huge makeshift plug. The second mate rammed the plug into the leak and sat with his feet on it to hold it in. They were just in time, for the boat was now very low in the sea. With boots, shoes and the bucket they scooped out the water until the boat was fairly dry.

Now they came upon the raft. The gunners were burning a Holmes light, but even if the lifeboat had not seen it they would have found the gunners from the noise they were making. Once the gunners were aboard, the empty raft was taken in tow behind the boat, for it might yet be needed in an emergency . . .

Aboard *Assyrian* they were busy launching the small liferafts, all they had left now that the half-submerged lifeboat had floated off, when suddenly the lifeless grey hulk of *Soesterberg* loomed out of the darkness. Though a smaller vessel, she seemed higher out of the water than *Assyrian?*

'Couldn't we board her?' Engineer Venables suggested to the captain.

Captain Kearon studied the drifting Dutchman.

'No,' he said, 'she's sinking - could go any time.'

On came the eerily floating Dutch ship to kiss very gently stern upon stern with the doomed *Assyrian*, as if in sympathy, before swinging away.

What followed shortly afterwards came as a cruel stroke of

fate. *Soesterberg*, still quite close, rose up by the bow a little and then slowly, like some stricken elephantine creature, reared up on end. Her bow thrust up almost vertically above the sea and she whined as she slid below the water. As she sank, thousands of pitprops burst from her holds and leapt high into the air, hurtling down again to skid across the surface of the sea and crash into the side of *Assyrian*. All the rafts were smothered, if not shattered, by the onslought.

Venables and one of the Commodore's naval telegraphists had just got away on one of the rafts when the cannonade of pitprops came smashing over the sea. Their raft was hit and began to break up. The telegraphist scrambled back on board *Assyrian*, now settled low in the water. Venables also tried to make a jump for the ship's side, but his hands were numb with cold and he missed, falling into the sea beneath the jostling pitprops. He struggled his way back to what remained of the smashed raft and made another attempt to reach the ship. This time a strong hand came over the ship's rail to help him aboard. It was the Commodore.

'All right, Second?'

Those now left on board were in a terrible plight. They had neither boats nor rafts. The ship's bow was submerged and she had an ominous list to port. The water made a mournful sound as it soughed up and down the alleyways.

Venables ran off and shone his torch down into the engine-room. Surprisingly, the water did not seem to have gained, and he began to have faint hopes that the ship might even yet remain afloat. He went on to look in the fiddley space and found a fireman dazedly sitting there, his jaw and arm broken. Venables called Steward Daley and together they gave the injured man rudimentary first-aid. They then secured him to a Board of Trade gangway, cut the lashings and let him float off, reasonably safe on his own personal raft.

There were about a dozen of them left on board now, including Captain Kearon, Commodore MacKinnon and two of his staff, the three Frenchmen, Daley, Venables, Radio Officer Stracy and the ship's carpenter. Captain Kearon called everyone together.

'Come on,' he said resolutely, 'we'll build our own raft . . .'

Under his prompt direction most of them now gathered under the poop and set to constructing a big raft out of painting planks and hatchboards. They were all soaking wet and their hands so cold they could hardly tie the knots to bind the raft together, but they started to joke and sing as they worked while the carpenter sawed the wood, even if at the back of their minds some were wondering what it would be like to die.

Commodore MacKinnon joined in, the soul of encouragement. His example, from a man nearing sixty, fired the younger ones among them with a cautious optimism. The main thing was to keep busy and not dwell on the horrible prospect of the drowning ship suddenly falling below the surface and dragging them all down with her.

Engineer Venables was hurrying off again to check the water level in the engine-room when he heard a voice calling his name from the sea. Looking across the moonlit mass of pitprops he could see Chief Officer King waving to him. King was hemmed in by pitprops some yards from the ship's side, and Venables ran for a rope to help him. But as he was doing so the wind and sea suddenly shifted the props and King was able to swim to the ship's side and clamber on board. For a moment the two men looked at each other, then as the absurdity of the situation mutually dawned on them they both laughed aloud . . . at the crazy notion that to them the deck of a sinking ship should appear as a place of safety.

Looking over the side now Venables saw the third engineer silently hanging on to a rope in the water. He lowered himself down to help the man, but could not unclasp the dead hands from the rope, for the man had expired even as he clung on.

Pulling himself back on board, Venables suddenly heard a voice calling for help. It came from the direction of the fiddley. He ran to it and his torch revealed the soot-smeared face of a young trimmer trapped beneath the top grating, his hands clenched on the rungs, his body below the shoulders immersed in dark, dusty water, a gash on his forehead bleeding into his eyes as he gazed pitiably up at the torchlight. Venables was doubly shocked to find the trapped man, as he had previously checked that no one was in the fiddley and nearly an hour had gone by since the ship was torpedoed. He called to Steward Daley, Radio Officer Robert Stracy, and a greaser named Bishop, to help him release the trimmer. Tenderly they laid him on the deck. He was terribly injured, his stomach torn open, his legs nearly off at the thighs. Stracy, a quiet man who normally could not bear to look at a cut finger, pushed back the man's spilling stomach and helped to apply a rough bandage. Daley placed a morphia tablet on the man's tongue and gave him some water. There was little else they could do except wrap him up warmly in blankets.

He was a Catholic youth from Liverpool's Scotland Road. As he lay suffering on the moonlit deck he kept moaning 'Holy Mary, Mother of God . . . Holy Mary . . .' He was to have been married when *Assyrian* docked. By rights he should never have been caught by the torpedo blast, for he was off-watch at the time and had only gone down to the stokehold for a chat with his mates.

A gangway lying on the deck nearby seemed a likely raft to carry both the injured man and his rescuers. They hauled it to the side of the ship and hoisted it over, preparatory to boarding it, but to their utter dismay it quickly sank.

Now two lifeboats could be seen rowing in the dark distance. They hailed them lustily, but a disappointing response came back across the water. 'We're full up mates,' and 'Sorry, we're sinking ourselves. . . .'

Unknown to them, one boat was from the *Soesterberg*, crammed full of men and towing the empty raft. Captain de Jong was faced with a dreadful dilemma. His leaking boat was fully loaded and he dared not pull too near *Assyrian* in case any men from her jumped overboard and tried to get into the boat, whereupon it would surely sink. All he could do was to row about wind, away from the ship, and release the raft so that it would float towards them. If some men could pick it up they would save themselves.

The other lifeboat, also unable to risk taking aboard a single extra man, was one from the *Empire Brigade*. . . .

The torpedo that tore into the starboard side of the *Empire Brigade*, a 6,000-ton vessel twice the size of *Assyrian*, blew a great hole in No. 2 hold at the side of the bridge.

Down in the radio cabin First Radio Officer Leonard Dewar, after picking up distress messages all night, had just remarked thankfully about their own ship 'Well, so far so good . . .' and was about to raise a hot drink to his lips when the torpedo struck.

'They've spilt my bloody cocoa!' he exclaimed indignantly. He tapped out 'No 53 torpedoed starboard side' and raced up to the bridge to report. Tall, balding Captain Parks was trying to assess the damage. There seemed no doubt that *Empire Brigade* had been fatally hit.

The captain and his officers now hurried down to the boatdeck to find that, incredibly, no lifeboats were left. The crew had gone without waiting for the order to abandon. One boat's painter had been chopped away and the boat launched with the way still on the ship.

A few men had not waited for the boats but dived straight over the side. One fireman-trimmer scrambled up the ladder from the engine-room and jumped into the sea to his death. Another casualty was the third engineer. Many times he had vowed 'If we're hit I won't trust you bastards to get me out - I'll trust to God to help me!' He did succeed in getting out of the engine-room after the explosion, but after having appeared on the boat-deck he was never seen again.

For the people scrambling down from the bridge there was no time to lose, as the ship's bow was already well down and her stern had risen high out of the water. Captain and everyone jumped overboard in the dark into the black sea. Radio Officer Dewar jumped from one of the Army lorries secured on the after deck, but no sooner had he jumped than he tried to get back, with the result that he slid heavily down the side of the ship, glimpsing the propeller still revolving in the air as he fell. He drifted away in the sea and was hit and knocked unconscious by an oar from one of the lifeboats, but they saw him and dragged him senseless into the boat.

All those from the bridge were eventually picked up by the lifeboats, though the captain himself was nearly lost. He was only spotted as he swam by his bald head shining in the moonlight.

Six men of the *Empire Brigade* lost their lives, either killed in the explosion or drowned, the big vessel sliding below the surface twenty minutes after being hit. . . .

On *Assyrian*, after unsuccessfully hailing the passing lifeboats, they were hurrying to get the makeshift raft ready for launching, but it looked doubtful whether it would carry everyone, even if it floated successfully. As time pressed, everything floatable on deck was flung overboard into the water in the hope that it might help to save a life. Engineer Venables and greaser Bishop even cut down the battered starboard lifeboat, still hanging by its one solitary fall. The boat fell into the water upside down. Bishop, together with a seaman and a fireman, sat on the capsized boat and made it fast to the ship's deck railing while Venables went back to the badly injured trimmer lying moaning on deck. He was now faced with the impossible task of getting the poor man across to the overturned boat. He searched around for some means of transporting him.

Meanwhile Chief Steward Daley, on going to the ship's rail, was surprised to see one of the small rafts put overboard earlier now floating intact only some twelve feet away from the ship's side. It was the kind of raft that carried a box containing biscuits and brandy. It was easy for Daley to reach, with lots of floating pitprops to help him and his Mae West life-jacket supporting him in the water. Manoeuvring the raft alongside the ship he called to the second steward, who came down and sat on the raft with his back to Daley's. They found it more difficult to get the raft away from the ship's side because the same helpful pitprops now hemmed them in, but they were joined by one of the Commodore's ratings and now the three of them, with the aid of a small piece of timber and by kicking out in the water, at last got clear. *Assyrian* now had almost no freeboard and was settling deeper every minute. They floated past the stern, where Captain Kearon, Commodore MacKinnon, Chief Officer King and at least three others were under the poop, still fighting against time to launch the raft.

Suddenly a tremor ran through the ship and it was clear she was going. 'Abandon ship!' cried the captain, and they began to push the makeshift raft over the stern. But even as they did so it began to break up. Hands had been too cold when tying the rope knots. Already the ship's stern was rising quickly out of the water. Men jumped from from the rail after the raft, one climbing down to the great propeller boss before jumping.

Away from the raft party Engineer Venables, in an agony of mind at having to leave the injured trimmer, had jumped hastily for the capsized boat. He and his three companions then shouted to let anyone who missed the raft know there was plenty of room for them on the keel of the boat. When no one answered they tried to push the boat away from the ship's side but could not, the suction of the sinking ship was holding it fast. Suddenly the ship's side seemed to jump up at them, the starboard davit swooped down through the air and sliced through the overturned boat between Bishop and Venables, who found themselves struggling underwater, fighting to free themselves from the pull of the ship.

Venables surfaced with difficulty, his skin scored by wires, his clothes torn and one leg of his trousers ripped to the thigh. He clutched his glasses to his eyes as he bobbed up, and saw the after part of *Assyrian* rear up above the sea. She stood on her bow, her twin screws high above, photographically etched against a moonlit cloud. He could see every plate of her, the sea grass vivid on her side. In front of him was the gaping black hole where the torpedo blast had ripped open her side, a frightening sight. He swam on his back away from it, deeply afraid of being sucked inside; he would have swum faster had he turned and used the breast-stroke, but he could not, for he was completely unable to drag his fascinated eyes away from the ship.

Assyrian hung poised for a moment above the water, and there was a tremendous crashing noise inside her, as if everything in the engine-room had broken loose. Then she slid beneath the dark surface of the sea, the displaced air from her holds droning through her ventilators like a mighty organ. And afterwards nothing, just a huge patch of frothing water, wreckage, and bales of cargo bobbing in the white foam as she sank to her grave more than a mile below.

The Germans had built *Assyrian*, and the Germans had sunk her.

There were voices now calling out from many directions, seeking comrades in the debris and dark. The raft, or what was left of it, had got away, but for several men a floating pitprop was their life-saver.

Commodore Lachlan MacKinnon never got on to the raft. As he struggled in the sea, his feet were grasped by Second Mate Frank Bellas and his head was held out of the water by Radio Officer Stracy, who hooked his arms through the Commodore's braces to tow him along until he had recovered sufficiently to strike out for himself. Stracy's own departure from the sinking vessel had had a touch of nonchalance about it. He simply walked off the vessel into the water, went down and down, and came up again with his uniform cap still firmly on his head.

Captain Kearon had floated off the ship and been sucked under as she plunged. A strong swimmer, he fought his way to the surface and came up beside a large spar to which Chief Officer King, nearly twice his age, was clinging for dear life. There was some rope trailing in the water and the captain used it to lash his elderly chief officer safely to the spar, after which he himself breasted the floating timber.

Now someone, somewhere in the dark, had burst bravely into song. It was the messroom steward, floating in the sea and singing in a discordant voice 'Roll Out The Barrel'. Elsewhere a seaman hanging on to a pitprop kept pulling something out of his jersey, waving it over his head and jubilantly shouting 'I've got my nylons!' Precious stockings for a girl friend, bought while in harbour at New York.

There was someone else half sitting up in the sea, holding on to a lifebuoy. It was Carrot, the Commodore's naval signaller. 'Are you okay?' someone called.

Cheerily Carrot replied, 'If it wasn't so bleeding cold it would be like being on the Serpentine!'

Soon men fell quiet as they floated aimlessly, and as the fitful moon came and went behind dark clouds they lost touch with one another and were left alone with their thoughts.

Steward Daley and his two companions on their small raft suddenly heard voices out of the silence, and looking in that direction saw a dark shape larger than themselves. They paddled and splashed their way across to it. The voices grew stronger, and the shape clearer. It was the port lifeboat, unbelievably still afloat on its tanks with only its occupants visible above the surface of the sea. Raft and boat drifted apart again and lost each other in the sea of pitprops. Everyone now was praying for daylight, and the chance of rescue. Could they stay afloat till then, and ward off the deadly effects of shock and exposure?

After the lifeboat had drifted on for some time there was great excitement when someone shouted 'Look - a destroyer!' Sure enough, about half a mile away there was something like a destroyer making straight towards them. But hearts dropped when, on coming closer, they found it was just another stricken merchant ship slowly sinking stern first.

Away across the sea of misery the occupants of Daley's raft now heard a lone voice calling out in a foreign tongue. They paddled towards it and found a seaman whom they judged to be a Greek. He grabbed Daley's side of the raft and hung on. Daley held on to him with one hand, and in doing so lost a briefcase containing the ship's articles and other papers which he had saved from his cabin and clung on to for so long; it spun away into the sea. It was impossible to pull the Greek up on to the raft, so Daley gave him some brandy and the man kept talking and talking, all quite unintelligible to them. He held on to Daley until the steward's arm was stiff and numb. With his free arm, Daley kept feeding the man brandy . . .

Engineer Bill Venables soon found himself swimming alone. He was fully dressed, complete with Merchant Navy muffler, rigged for a night in a boat or on a raft, not for swimming the Atlantic. He tried to take his shoes off to give himself more freedom, but the water had tightened the laces and his hands were too cold to undo them. His life-jacket was nearly in shreds after his struggle to escape when the *Assyrian* rolled over on top of him. For more than an hour now he swam alone with a pitprop under each arm. He came upon dead men floating facedown in their life-jackets and turned them over to see if he recognized them. But there was no companionship even from the dead for they were all strange faces from other ships.

The water did not seem as cold as he thought it would be, but his hands soon lost all feeling and his stomach felt as if it was full of ice. He began to fear that even if he was eventually picked up he would be a physical wreck for the rest of his life.

Coming upon some packing cases floating in the sea he tried to climb up on to them, but as he did so the cases simply rolled over on top of him and pushed him under the water. He went back to the support of his pitprops.

Suddenly a new fear shot through him as he saw a periscope skimming along through the moonlight. The U-boat's conning-tower was almost awash and he thought it was going to surface. He hid behind a floating bale, greatly afraid of being taken prisoner, and to his intense relief the grim shape of the U-boat passed on.

As the time dragged on, the icy feeling in his stomach crept higher, and he felt that when it reached his heart he would die. The moon was lowering behind the scudding clouds and he was afraid it would vanish altogether, leaving him in darkness. He seemed to be the only thing that lived on the face of the sea.

Lived? He was as good as dead already, for they could none of them reasonably hope to be rescued at all. The surviving merchant ships had all gone on, and no doubt the escorts with them, for warships could not stop to search for men in the sea while the enemy still threatened. This they all knew.

Suddenly the awfulness of his situation was too much. Very deliberately, Bill Venables put his head under water and tried to drown himself, but found he could not do it . . .

In another part of the sea another lonely survivor clung forlornly to a supporting piece of timber. It was Commodore MacKinnon. After recovering from the first shock of immersion he had lost touch with his rescuers and swam alone for some distance before finding a small raft with six men sitting or lying on it. It was loaded to danger point, clearly unable to support another body, so he found a plank of wood for support and held on to the raft, adamantly refusing to board it in spite of the entreaties of its occupants, in case he should sink them all.

He clung on to the raft as long as he could, but as the numbness crept through his limbs he had to let go of it and drift away on his plank. Now he floated as the waters took him, feeling for the first time the full weight of his fifty-seven years. But it was not his growing physical distress and horror at being alone in the dark that finally drove through to his heart, it was the hopeless situation of everyone who might still be bobbing precariously on the littered surface of the sea.

His convoy had been massacred. His own ship had gone, and

the Vice-Commodore ship, *Scoresby*, had been sunk long before. Any merchant ships that survived now had no merchant leader, nor, as far as he knew, any escorts.

As he floated on his life-saving piece of timber with all hopes of rescue fading, he mercifully could not know that the slaughter of SC7 was far from done.

When *Leith* and *Fowey*, racing hard for the convoy shortly after midnight, saw flashes on the starboard horizon and set course towards them, they came upon the big Glasgow ship *Blairspey*, loaded high with timber, stopped and drifting after being rocked by a torpedo blast.

Aboard *Blairspey*, her crew all either Scotsmen or Northerners, the night had seen a certain change among the engine-room staff. Beforehand when the convoy was quiet, her stokers had gone down to the stokehold to pitch, slice and rake the boiler fires, then returned to sit in the galley, deeming it to be safer there. But as the events of the night plunged them into the thick of danger the same men had stayed working like fury in the stokehold, not only those on duty but others off-watch, stoking up the fires to give *Blairspey* the steam she needed in her efforts to speed away from the enemy. She had thumped and dodged through the night at a rate she was not originally designed for, doing a good twelve knots with all safety valves closed down. But it was not enough. With her wheel hard over to port, she was torpedoed in No. 1 hold, port side, and quickly came to a stop, blowing off steam very hard.

In a moment of panic the starboard lifeboat was let down into the water, but Captain J. C. ('Jesus Christ') Walker, a Glasgow man like all the ship's officers, firmly ordered the boat to be re-hoisted. There was no question of abandoning ship, he declared, until the ship abandoned them.

It was then that *Leith*'s signal lamp winked across the water. 'Are you in trouble?'

Captain Walker signalled back that he was confident *Blairspey* could keep afloat and that he could steam her at six knots independently.

Leith replied that she was sorry she could not stand by but would try to send an escort shortly. Then off she vanished after *Fowey*, still trying to catch up with the convoy.

Only twenty minutes after the sloop's departure *Blairspey* shuddered and reeled in the water again as a second torpedo struck her, this time on her starboard side in No. 2 hold. It was the end. Captain Walker ordered abandon ship.

The captain took one lifeboat with nineteen members of the crew, and they got clean away in the darkness. Chief Officer John Glasgow took the other boat with the remaining thirteen men, including Second Radio Officer John Crawford. They were not so lucky. Being on the port side, the windward side, they had difficulty pulling away from the stricken ship. They were still trying to get clear when a third torpedo hit *Blairspey* port side under the bridge. The fierce explosion blew timber high into the air and it came raining down into the sea, bouncing up again from the surface in all directions. The lifeboat fortunately escaped the flying timber but was thrown back on its beam by the surging water, hurling several men into the sea. Yet by some miracle no one was injured, and the men thrown into the sea were pulled back to safety.

The two lifeboats never joined each other. Far across the water, in the captain's boat, there was panic when a U-boat was spotted on the surface making directly for them. It came close and almost stopped, and there was a cold fear of spraying machine-guns.

'What ship?' asked the German commander.

'*Blairspey*,' replied Captain Walker.

Satisfied, the U-boat sped on into the night.

Twenty-five miles due south of the now silently drifting *Blairspey*, in an area of ocean covering some thirty square miles, the relentless destruction of SC7's scattered ships continued.

The small Norwegian steamer *Snefjeld* sank quickly when a torpedo tore a hole in her side. The thirty-nine year old vessel just seemed to fall apart, even her timber cargo could not keep her afloat.

The British *Sedgepool* was three times as big as the old *Snefjeld*, but again one torpedo was enough. The explosion blew away a wing of the bridge, killing the captain and his second officer - they simply vanished. Death also struck down in the engine-room, where the third engineer died instantly. The main wireless aerial broke adrift and part of it hung over the ship's funnel, while the emergency aerial was blown clean away.

Chief Engineer James Aves shut down the ship's engines and came on deck to find that he was left absolutely alone on a derelict vessel - the lifeboats had gone, except for one which had jammed at the side of the ship and been abandoned. Desperately he tried to free the boat, but in doing so he badly crushed his hand. He gave up and jumped overboard, having to swim around for some time before being picked up by a few of the crew who had got away on a raft. Later they were all taken aboard one of the ship's lifeboats. As they pulled away in the dark they could see the ship, loaded with grain, settling in the water but still well afloat.

Fifteen miles to the south the Greeks of the old *Thalia*, carrying a full load of steel to Liverpool, were not so fortunate. The big steamer, nearly 6,000-tons, sank almost as soon as she was hit. There were no survivors.

At this time the still floating *Shekatika*, drifting far to the rear, shook with the impact of a third torpedo delivered by a third U-boat. This third explosion was too much, even with her great packing of timber. Wood spewing from the big holes in her sides, *Shekatika* settled rapidly in the water.

And now, headlong into the most southerly area of attack by the wolf-pack, steamed the *Clintonia*, the Stag Line ship carrying pulpwood for Manchester. Captain Thomas Irvin had seen all five vessels leading their columns on his port side receive direct hits. One of them was the *Assyrian*, which had left *Clintonia* a 'sitting duck' and the convoy without a leader. After the loss of the Commodore ship a speaker for the officers and crew told Captain Irvin they were prepared to go it alone; that is, to sail independently, which *Clintonia* had been doing all the time up to joining SC7. Having had a brief gun battle with a U-boat on the outward voyage and got the better of the exchange, the crew believed they could now stand up to anything they could see. With these reassurances Captain Irvin set course away from the convoy's planned route in the hope of clearing well out of the area by daybreak.

But it was not to be. At 3 a.m., having run the gauntlet for the past two hours without sight or sound of the enemy, the master was remarking to his second officer on the bridge how lucky he felt, when they sighted a U-boat close to port. So close, in fact, that had there been a hand grenade on the bridge he could have lobbed it down the German's conning-tower. *Clintonia*'s gun-crew scrambled to their station as the klaxon horn gave the alarm.

Captain Irvin skilfully brought the German astern and ordered his gun-crew to open fire. But even in the moonlight they could not see anything to fire at, probably because they were so much lower than the bridge. One shot might have stopped the U-boat; instead, the chance was missed. There now commenced a taut battle of hide and seek as Captain Irvin swung his ship first this way and then that to confuse the German, always trying to get into a position from which his gun-crew could get in a shot.

The duel in the dark went on for nearly an hour, until, as one particular manoeuvre developed between the two vessels, it suddenly dawned on Captain Irvin that this time *he* was the mouse, having been very neatly lured into a position of attack not from his immediate adversary but from a second U-boat moving in from another direction. Too late the master ordered his ship to swing away, for with the U-boat he had been watching still well visible astern, a torpedo from the other German streaked for *Clintonia*'s port side.

The resultant explosion blew the mainmast clean out of the ship - it came crashing down on the wireless cabin, smashing the cabin and all equipment, making it impossible to send a distress message. The blast swept right across the ship, throwing the breech worker of the four-inch gun, the chief cook, head first into the open breech, his head being forced into the gun barrel and terribly crushed.

The master and chief engineer hurried to the top of the engine-room and on looking down saw that the water was up to the cylinders. There was no other recourse but to abandon ship. The ship's secret papers were dumped overboard and the two lifeboats launched, Chief Officer Buglass taking one boat and the captain the other, the captain including the badly injured cook in his company. They had scarcely got clear of the ship before a second torpedo crashed into her. Again she shivered hugely under an explosion which blew the whole of her bridge high into the air, but still her 3,000 tons remained afloat on her pulpwood cargo. She was doomed, but would take her own time to sink.

Now the first U-boat, the one *Clintonia* had been duelling with, approached and started to shell the ship. It was an incredible scene to the watchers in the lifeboats, like two dogs fighting over a bone; the second U-boat had to retire hurriedly out of the line of fire to escape being hit. So had the lifeboats, for the German gun-crew seemed very erratic with their shooting, three shells whistling a few feet above the boats and sending all hands diving flat to the boards for safety. Grabbing the oars afterwards they pulled hard out of range. The U-boat kept firing away as if determined to shoot off every last bit of the ship's deck cargo. They counted twenty-three shells before its gun was silent.

There was another explosion from *Clintonia*, this time the boiler going up. The mauled ship then began to go down by the stern, rearing up to a vertical position before disappearing from sight in a whirlpool of debris.

The lifeboats had to scatter quickly again as the cargo of

pulpwood rushed up to the surface and shot dangerously out of the water over a large area. One hit would have been enough to hole a boat and spill its occupants into the sea.

Lost from each other now, each boat made its separate plans. The captain decided to lay his boat to a sea anchor till daylight. They did what they could for the gravely injured cook, the captain cushioning him gently between his legs to steady him from the rocking motion of the boat, for the sea was getting up. But the cook died as he sat there. Quietly, when the rest of the boat's occupants were lying down trying to get some rest, the captain, helped by the second officer and the chief steward, cast the poor man's mutilated body to the deep.

Clintonia was the last victim of the wolf-pack, but while she was fighting her desperate duel other human dramas were being enacted across the sea to her rear.

Leith, steaming hard in the wake of the scattered convoy, finally arrived at the centrepoint of destruction where the Commodore ship, together with *Soesterberg* and *Empire Brigade*, had gone down. Faced now with the problem of whether to continue at speed after the remnants of the convoy or to stop and save what life he could, Commander Allen decided there was only one reasonable course of action he could take. It was a decision he would amply justify later on the grounds that the remaining ships of the convoy must now be so scattered that the chances of immediately finding any of them were remote, also the U-boats attacking in the area must surely have expended all their torpedoes. Accordingly *Leith* began her mercy work.

Elated survivors of *Assyrian*, seeing with salt stung eyes the glad sight of the sloop ghosting over the debris-strewn sea in the moonlight, raised hoarse cries and cheers as she neared them, but the shouts died away in their throats when she steamed on and deliberately passed them by. The men in the water could not believe their eyes, and on realizing that she was indeed leaving them behind, the night air rang with their desperate yells and vivid curses. Commodore MacKinnon, swimming alone, had also seen the approach of the sloop and, as she steamed on and away, bowed his head over his supporting pitprop. He knew that officially she should not stop but pursue the enemy to the limits, and she was only doing her duty. So this was the end of them.

Then suddenly *Leith* was back and slowing down to save them all from the sea. She had had to make an asdic sweep of the area first, and now her crew worked fast, for when stopped the ship was an easy target for any lurking U-boat. Commander Allen paced agonisingly back and forth on the bridge, frequently stressing the need for speed in forceful language to the first lieutenant supervising operations in the waist. Rescue nets hung down over both sides of the quarter-deck, lifelines were thrown to men swimming, boathooks were busy pulling in anything that floated to see if it held a survivor. When some survivors attempted to climb the nets they found they had lost the use of their legs; *Leith*'s willing sailors climbed down the nets to help the exhausted men up.

From the decks of *Leith* it was a terrible scene made all the more grotesque by the coldly shining light of the moon, the sea littered with wreckage, pitprops, oil, and yelling and screaming men frightened that they might not be seen and left to die.

Steward Daley and his two companions were saved from their raft, but the Greek seaman he had hung on to in the water for so long died soon after being pulled on board, and was returned to the sea. All the men in the waterlogged port lifeboat were saved and several others were picked up out of the sea, including Second Mate Bellas, who was hanging on to a pitprop, and Captain Kearon. There were cheers from the soaking, bedraggled survivors for their popular master as he was helped aboard, but it was a moment of tragedy, too, for Chief Officer King, still lashed to the spar as the master had tried to save him, had died from exposure. His body was left to drift away in the water. Another man who had clung to the same piece of timber had also died just before rescue came, and now slipped away and sank in the sea.

When Engineer Bill Venables, still swimming alone, saw the dark shape of the sloop ahead of him he could hardly believe it was real, and not just a feverish dream. Silhouetted as she was, the searching ship seemed to have come straight out of the moon.

'Ahoy there!' he cried, and an unmistakably live voice immediately answered. He cried out again, and the same voice gave him encouragement - 'Keep calling! Keep calling!' They could not see him from the sloop but his voice told them his direction.

When *Leith* drew closer Venables abandoned his life-saving pitprops and threshed through the water like a madman towards her. He saw a lifebelt drop into the sea beside him, thankfully grabbed it and pulled it over his head. Then something snapped inside him and he was pulled on board near senseless.

Five others helped out of the water were injured. One fireman's ribs had been broken by a pounding pitprop, yet he had found the strength to swim on.

Weakly, from some distance away in the sea, the horrified Commodore saw a torpedo speed pointblank for *Leith*. But there was no explosion. The torpedo passed harmlessly underneath her, being set deep for a merchant ship. Minutes later they had found him, but he was totally unable to swim to his rescuers, so they lowered a net and hoisted him up inside it. As he rose into the air, water streaming from him, he was accidentally upended, and even as he swung there he could appreciate the wry humour of the situation. So many times over so many years had he boarded naval ships being accorded the full honours befitting his senior rank; now here he was being hoisted aboard like a sack of potatoes.

More tragic discoveries were made of floating bodies, which were left to drift away in the water. One was the injured firemen who had been sent floating away from *Assyrian* secured on a gangway; when found to be dead he was cast away again on his bizarre funeral craft to go bobbing across the night ocean to eternity.

Now came further horror when the searching sloop came upon a small raft with one man sitting on it. He had a broken arm and was holding on tightly with his sound arm. They tried repeatedly to get near enough to him in the dark to throw him a line, but he would not let go with his good arm to try to get the line, and every time the ship went astern to lose way, the wash from her propellers swept him away out of range. There were no other men in the water near enough to help him, and *Leith* could not remain stopped for too long. Eventually, after many tries, she had to move across to pick up more survivors farther away, leaving the unfortunate man on his raft, alone.

When the count came to be made, nearly half of *Assyrian*'s company had been lost, including one of the Commodore's petty officers and the young ship's carpenter who had worked so hard to build the raft. And of those now rescued, one seaman and the Commodore's yeoman of signals were both critically ill.

Now there were more shouts in the night as the sloop came upon the survivors of *Soesterberg* . . .

The Dutch ship's leaky lifeboat had stayed afloat on its plugging of socks. All the men who were soaking wet had been put in the rear of the boat, where they huddled together under blankets taken from the boat's blanket box. The boat's sail was spread over them, too, so that the body warmth of each man would help the others.

They had first had a good swig of brandy. At first Second Mate Ort had refused because he was a teetotaller. But Captain de Jong told him 'Ort, this is not alcohol, this is medicine which the doctor prescribes.'

'Then I'll take it,' said the mate obediently, 'as medicine I could never refuse.' He took a good swallow - and said afterwards that if all medicine tasted that good he would take it regularly.

After a long time in the boat they suddenly saw white foam from a good distance away, and then something black came out of the darkness at speed towards them. It was *Leith*. The sloop had spotted them from the white sail spread over the wet crew, and when she was near they could hear the sound of the ship's telegraph. The powerful engines were hard in reverse, and her commander worked them so that the rear part, where the climbing nets hung overboard, was exactly at the height of the lifeboat.

'Hurry up!' shouted Commander Allen from the bridge.

His call was unnecessary, for the men who had been unable to bale out the lifeboat to stop it sinking now burst into life and were the first on the warship's deck. Captain de Jong watched them more in sorrow than in anger. He himself climbed aboard carrying the bag with his ship's secret papers, but without the still half full bottle of brandy, which he forgot in the hurry, much to his regret as he had not had time to take a drop himself.

Away went *Leith* to find more survivors. This time they were from the *Empire Brigade*, in various states of exhaustion and some covered in filthy oil. With them was a stoker from *Soesterberg* who had been pitched overboard by the enormous water column thrown up when the ship was torpedoed, but who had managed to keep afloat on two pitprops. Encountering a boat of the British survivors he had clung on to the boat with one arm until it slipped completely out of socket without him noticing it. No sooner had he climbed on to *Leith*'s deck than he dropped unconscious.

Leith continued her systematic search but found only wreckage and bodies. Nothing else living and no sign of the enemy. She now had the survivors of four ships aboard her, including the Estonians from the *Nora*, and resembled a floating casualty station. The wardroom, messdecks and passages were crowded with sprawling bodies, the ship's doctor and his assistant going from one man to another to attend to their medical needs. All the blankets, towels and clothing that could be spared were given to the survivors to keep them warm. For many of them the night ended there, as they slept the sleep of exhaustion. Like Radio Officer Dewar of *Empire Brigade*, who, wet and reeking with oil, fell asleep on the wardroom floor and when he awoke, found he had been covered with Captain de Jong's overcoat. The kindly Dutch master had gone off to look for a warm place to sleep in the engine-room. He found it, but after a few hours bedded down on a metal platform his body really ached and the form of the 'iron toaster' was imprinted on his body.

Engineer Venables, who had collapsed from exposure, was taken to the galley and massaged for an hour before he showed signs of life, after which it took the full strength of two of his rescuers to restrain him as he struggled to get at the galley fire. He was fed hot cocoa, and knew no more till he awoke with a scalded throat, to find himself wrapped in blankets on the mess-deck and a friendly Greek sailor lying beside him trying to put a cigarette in his mouth. They were crowded under low lighting and there was the whine of forced ventilation. Eventually some-one discovered that Venables was an officer and his uniform was brought from the engine-room where it had been drying. He joined the officer survivors in the wardroom, where the hugely smiling features of Queen Salote looked down on the scene from a photograph on the bulkhead.

Chief Steward Daley, on regaining the use of his legs, went through the crowded alleyways searching for fellow survivors of *Assyrian*, and was glad to find them. Arriving back at the galley he was handed a cup of steaming cocoa and was surprised to see *Assyrian*'s cooks busy with two huge frying pans, making pan-cakes. Sailors, probably lookouts and gun-crews, took it in turns to appear and collect a cup of cocoa and a pancake dipped in sugar. They were very tired but showed their genuine appreciation, if it was only to say 'Thanks, scouse,' or 'There's nothing like working your passage, mates . . .'

Commodore MacKinnon had been hauled aboard feeling the certain ill effects of long exposure. They got a hot drink into him, stripped him down and tried to rub him unnumbed, but he could not stop shivering. They wanted to bundle him off to bed, but he refused, saying he would just sleep in a chair. The situation called for a bit of naval strategy. After a quiet word with the ship's doctor Commander Allen insisted that he wanted to turn in but could not do so until the Commodore had done so, at which they finally got the admiral to bed in blankets and there he stayed, in the commander's sleeping cabin.

In the meantime *Fowey* had also been searching for survivors, but without any luck, as she steamed over the route of the convoy. But for *Bluebell*, standing by as dawn came, rescue operations began all over again. First, she found the captain's boat from *Blairspey* with its nineteen occupants, then the two boats from *Beatus*, whose survivors had been drifting for some ten hours since their ship sank. It had been difficult for them to row with all the pitprops and wreckage around, and the best they could do was to get to the windward of the floating mess, in order to avoid damage to the boats. Had help not arrived they would have eventually hoisted sail and tried to make it for home.

Although it was now daylight, the work of getting the survivors aboard *Bluebell* was even trickier than it had been during the night. The wind had freshened and the sea was anything but gentle, requiring great patience and skill to get the corvette alongside the lifeboats. Survivors already aboard willingly helped the sailors with the rescue work, and as before, the boats were emptied of anything useful, from blankets to lifeboat biscuits in tins firmly stamped 'Spillers'. Then the plugs were taken out of the boats and they were left to drift away and sink among the wreckage which still dotted the surface of the ocean as far as the eye could see.

It was 8.25 a.m. when *Bluebell* wirelessed the Commander-in-Chief, Western Approaches, that she had now picked up the captain and eighteen crew of *Blairspey* and the captain and thirty-six crew of *Beatus*, adding the startling message: 'Have now on board 203 survivors. Am rejoining convoy.'

But there was no longer any convoy to rejoin. The surviving ships had all scattered far and wide in a wind-whipped sea growing rougher by the minute.

One of the scattered vessels was the scrap-carrier *Corinthic*, in which Radio Officer Kenneth Howell had been keeping a diary since the start of the voyage. Day by day, for his wife's eyes only, he had entered events in a cheap school exercise book, the kind with arithmetic tables printed at the back. But his entry for the past night was a single paragraph. As *Corinthic*'s pounding engines took her safely away from the scene of slaughter he wrote from the heart.

'Of the events that have taken place during the last few hours of this "Black Friday" I will write again if we are spared to get through this next day and night. Suffice to say at present that I was never so glad and thankful that during these months I have been back at sea I have each day said my prayers as I have been in the habit of at home. I am sure that during the last twenty-four hours only something higher than any good fortune has enabled us to be still sailing on this Saturday morning. For which fact I shall always return thanks.'

10

The Bottomless *Bluebell*

For five hours after picking up her last survivors, *Leith* steamed at her top speed of sixteen knots over the course of the convoy route, scouring the roughening sea for surviving ships. But depressingly she found none. At 9.30 a.m. on Saturday morning, October 19, the sloop reduced speed to fourteen knots to ease her racing engines.

Commander Allen continued to scan the grey sea through his glasses. He was now painfully aware, from his own observations and such scraps of information as he had been able to glean from survivors, that SC7 had been the victim of a well organized attack by the Germans. From the positions of some of the stricken ships, the times at which they were attacked, and the number of torpedoes known to have been fired, allowing for near misses, it seemed clear that at least two U-boats, perhaps three, had taken part in the assault.

The surprise had been complete and devastating. The three escorts had been rendered powerless by the U-boats' surface tactics, which were entirely unexpected. It had all been a gigantic mess, with each fighting vessel forced instead to take on the role of rescue ship – it had been a case of either doing that or leaving hundreds of men to the mercies of the sea. Now, on this rough morning, some ships at least should still be sailing . . . some must have escaped destruction. But where were they? The empty ocean gave no clue.

The ship's doctor came to the bridge with some bad news. Commodore MacKinnon, suffering acutely from the effects of exposure, had not stopped shivering since his rescue, and his condition had gradually deteriorated. Now the worst had happened. There were signs of pneumonia in his right lung.

The next few hours were a grim challenge for Surgeon-Lieutenant John Robertson, RN, as he struggled to save the admiral's life. A young doctor not long out of Edinburgh University, he tried all he knew to arrest the pneumonia, but the Commodore's condition worsened until he had clearly reached the point of death. There was a gurgling in his throat and he was at his last gasp. At this desperate moment young Robertson took the only gamble left open to him He had a supply of the new 'M and B 693' tablets, the specially developed drug now being issued to the Services. The tablets were so new that Robertson had not himself used them before, nor knew anybody who had, and he had no idea of the prescribed dose for such a case. Calmly, but with a silent prayer, he administered the tablets to the dying patient, deliberately erring on the side of feeding him too much of the drug rather than too little.

No one, least of all the doctor himself, was quite prepared for what happened next. Only half an hour after being given the tablets the Commodore seemed to rally round, and an hour later he was definitely more peaceful, though still very dangerously ill.

Inspired by the miraculous change in his patient, pulled back from death's door, Robertson began to see a glimmer of hope. 'The Commodore is in a very bad way,' he told the captain, 'but with a little luck we should get him home.'

He would see to it. The young doctor was never more determined.

The good news found its way down among the crew and some of the host of survivors, giving rise to hopes that the other two sick men from *Assyrian* now fighting for their lives might yet be saved.

Among the sailors of *Leith* anger was intense at the slaughter of the convoy, for it seemed obvious to them that the U-boats had worked to a plan and cleverly lain in wait for SC7. The naval men's anger was directed at the continuing situation whereby U-boats appeared to be allowed sanctuary off the southern Irish coast, roaming ready to strike at incoming convoys at will, while the Irish Republic remained stubbornly neutral and overrun with German spies. British warships and planes, denied southern Irish bases, were severely handicapped, yet despite all the carnage at sea the British Government seemed powerless to do anything about it. Why?

Anger was something the survivors themselves were not capable of at this time. They could only feel a numbed relief. Even the thought of the usual remarks from the 'well informed' among the civilian population that would greet them once again when, and if, they reached home, for the present held no bitterness . . . 'Oh, but *you* are all right in the Merchant Navy . . .'

Men sat or lay as they could among clothes hung everywhere to dry, and papers, wallets and paper money also laid out to dry off. They clung to whatever meagre possessions they had managed to save from the sea. There was the mate of one vessel who sat or lay on his sextant, his only saved possession, the whole time, and would not let anyone come near it. All deck officers prized their sextants and the loss was all the greater when, as in one instance, the sextant was new and fitted with micrometer reading and small built-in light. Some other survivors had saved their 'sub bags', but many had only the sea-soaked contents of their pockets. Engineer Bill Venables thought sadly of his own possession taken down to the ocean depths by *Assyrian*. The beech and mahogany propeller for his Flying Flea, on which he had lavished so much work, was hanging over his bunk when she sank. It was not unusual for a man to think of his lost belongings at such a time. Down, like everyone else's, had gone Commodore MacKinnon's precious personal things. In clearer moments he would think of them. Everything gone. The little presents he had been bringing home for his wife and daughter in Britain, the fountain pen he treasured, his pipes, and the comfortable old slippers he had worn for years, steadfastly refusing to allow anyone to buy him new ones . . .

At noon, in worsening weather, *Leith* steamed on following a high easterly course level on an invisible line with the southernmost Hebrides. Commander Allen now wirelessed Western Approaches Command and reported the number of survivors he had picked up, including the Commodore, who was on board in a critical condition. 'Have not found any other ships of the convoy,' the message added. 'Am joining *Fowey* . . .'

But in fact Allen would never sight his fellow escort again.

Commander Aubrey, after searching unsuccessfully for more survivors, had kept *Fowey* steaming on a more southerly course than *Leith*, and at daybreak he was rewarded with the sight of first one ship, then another . . . and another, until excitedly they counted eight scattered vessels in all. Eight ships! Survivors on *Fowey*'s decks gladdened at the cheering sight, waving vigorously at the plodding shapes of vessels they had become familiar with during the long voyage but had never expected to see again.

Commander Aubrey now set about reforming the eight scattered ships into a miniature convoy less than a quarter of the size of the one that had set out from Sydney so long ago. A Commodore ship had to be appointed to lead them, but there was little ceremony attached to this, it was simply a case of choosing either the biggest vessel among them, or the one out ahead. The *Somersby*, the West Hartlepool ship of more than 5,000 tons, fitted the bill admirably. *Fowey*'s morse lamp blinked across the rising seas, and *Somersby*'s radio officer was called to the bridge to help Captain Bill Thompson translate the message and signal their reply by hand torch. And that was that. Captain Thompson, a Cardiff master who had raced *Somersby* to safety by screwing down the safety valves and raising a shuddering ten knots, now took the lead as Commodore ship.

As the weather continued to worsen there was little opportunity for the members of the convoy to take much stock of one another, but it was enough that they were now all together, in fair order, and with *Fowey* to screen them as best she could. Their position was actually some forty miles south-west of *Leith* when close to noon, Commander Aubrey wirelessed Western Approaches Command to report that he had rounded up eight ships of convoy SC7 and was escorting them in at a speed of seven and a half knots. He added that he estimated some ten ships of SC7 had been torpedoed . . .

In fact the full terrible total of ships sunk during the night was sixteen. Together with the four ships lost earlier, SC7 had lost twenty ships; well over half the convoy.

It was at this time that the sloop Scarborough, *coming up in the rear more than eighty miles to the north-west, passed through the area where* Assyrian *and others had gone down. All that remained now was some sea tossed wreckage and an empty, aimlessly drifting lifeboat. There were no signs of survivors.*

In the mid-afternoon, when the black stormy weather was already beginning to merge with evening darkness, the lonesomely steaming *Leith* was relieved to sight the *Heartsease*, still escorting the damaged *Carsbreck*. In all the chaos of the past night, the corvette had stood close by her crippled charge as they steamed through a sea of debris and occasional empty lifeboats, with smoke palls spiralling on the horizon to mark the fate of the convoy ahead of them. *Carsbreck* now was very much down by the bow, but still pushing slowly ahead in ungainly fashion with her mainmast leaning drunkenly in two directions at once, and timber still escaping every now and then from the great hole in her side.

Three other scattered ships of the convoy had come upon the corvette and her charge and were now keeping close company with them. One was the small Norwegian *Inger Elisabeth*, an other was the *Corinthic*. A forlorn sight, this small handful of remnants. *Leith* steamed ahead of the five vessels, leading them on into the wild evening seas. The wind had reached gale force, with the darkening sky heavily overcast, and frequent squalls of lashing rain making visibility poor.

In the late afternoon a distant rumbling explosion was clearly heard between decks aboard *Leith*. Half an hour later came the tremors of another explosion. What was happening now? And where?

In his bunk the sick Commodore trembled at the noises. Every time the sloop banged down in the rough weather he thought, in his fever, that it was another torpedo.

Far to the south, as *Fowey*'s convoy of eight ships strove to keep their stations in the ever worsening seas, a familiar nauseating voice came over the ships' radios. 'Jairmany calling, Jairmany calling . . .' Convoy SC7 had been smashed, said Lord Haw-Haw - it was a great and glorious victory for the German U-boats. He went on to describe how the U-boats had beaten the convoy's 'destroyer' escorts and 'pulverized' the merchant ships in a daring night attack . . . But on many of the ships now listening, Haw-Haw's final words were lost in a torrent of jeers and abuse. Aboard the old *Botusk*, such was the richly inventive language used against the English traitor, consigning him to highly imaginative ends, that the like had never been heard before on that ship, nor would be again. Unwittingly, far from being the voice of doom, Haw-Haw was the greatest booster of British morale.

But they steamed on into a dreadful night. The thick squally weather reduced visibility to vanishing point, while a tearing gale whipped ship after ship off her station. For the *Botusk* it was a night of high danger as she nearly ran ashore on the north-west coast of Ireland. Only when they managed to obtain a 'fix' and by dead reckoning retraced their movements did they realize the narrowness of their escape.

Through all the worst of the night *Fowey* managed to keep company with the lead ship of the centre column, but when dawn broke on Sunday, October 20, it disclosed a very changed scene. *Fowey* and her companion found themselves completely alone on a tossing sea, every other vessel of the small convoy having been blown away in the night. It was useless searching for them now. Commander Aubrey decided that his best course of action, with his ship crammed with a hundred and fifty-seven survivors, was to make for an early port; so instead of setting course for Liverpool he planned to steam for the Clyde and try to land the survivors there before darkness. At 10 a.m. he wirelessed these intentions to Western Approaches Command, and *Fowey* sped on her way.

Leith had not been any more fortunate in battling her way through the foul conditions of the night. During the turbulent small hours she lost touch with *Heartsease* and the four merchantmen, and at daylight found herself alone again on a still angry sea. At noon, with still no other ships in sight, Commander Allen wirelessed Western Approaches Command that he was now coming in to land survivors. Unlike *Fowey*, however, he would steam direct to Liverpool.

Late that afternoon aboard *Leith* they witnessed a final sad epitaph to SC7. The two seriously ill men from *Assyrian*, the Commodore's yeoman of signals and a seaman, had both died. Their canvas-wrapped bodies were laid side by side, covered with the red and white ensigns, the burial service was read, the shots fired, and the bodies were slid over the stern.

So many other shipmates who had died had not known these honours. The ceremony, in its way, remembered them all.

The corvette *Bluebell*, after her long hours of rescue work, steamed on but never sighted another ship. Crowded to capacity with survivors, Commander Sherwood decided there was nothing else for it but to get back to the U.K. as soon as possible.

As the corvette did not carry any medical personnel no one knew how to attend to the injured, some of whom ended up swathed in bandages like mummies. But there were no serious cases, and they got by. Of more immediate concern in the cramped conditions prevailing were men who were as sick as a dog for twenty-four hours or more owing to the different, and more violent, motion of the corvette compared with that of a merchantman.

Bluebell was now in the fantastic position of having four times as many survivors as crew. The naval men gave up everything they could to them. Two weary *Empire Miniver* officers were eternally grateful to the sailor who turned over his bunk to them - how they ever managed to climb into it to sleep there together they never knew, but sleep they did. Later, when all ships' officers were requested to move into the wardroom, the two regretfully left their 'comfortable' quarters and moved into the small and overcrowded officers' accommodation where everyone was obliged to spend most of the time sitting on the deck.

All the masters were gathered in the captain's cabin, where Captain Brett of *Beatus* and Captain Weatherill of *Scoresby* tossed up for Commander Sherwood's bunk. Weatherill won. He was the lucky one, the remainder having to share the deck space between them.

But all these were small nuisances against the one great problem: food. The escort corvettes were only stored for ten days, plus a small surplus for emergencies, and with so many mouths to feed the 'winnings' from the lifeboats added little to the general supply. So food had to be strictly rationed, both crew and survivors sharing the same meagre menu. However, it was all done in orderly fashion. In the wardroom it may have been only ship's biscuits and corned beef, but it was correctly served at the table.

Bluebell steamed on through heavily overcast weather. Then she ran into fog, which really placed them in an impossible situation. They had not seen the sun for days, and Commander Sherwood was sailing his ship a little by guess and by God. Every officer survivor aboard - and there were some thirty of them - tried to help by pitching in with his calculations, but none could find the sun to take a sight; except one, Chief Officer Coultas of *Scoresby*, who, to the commander's lasting amusement, swore that he had. However, the blunt truth of their position came out of the murk later when they sighted Tory Island, off north-west Ireland, on the wrong bow. *Bluebell* had been running 'blind' to the south.

But now Commander Sherwood could set course for home at *Bluebell*'s best speed. Everything would be all right now, he assured his 'guests', and they could all go to sleep, for if they slept they would eat less food. He was not joking, for the rapidly diminishing food supply was his major worry. He decided they would have to make for the nearest point to land the survivors, so headed *Bluebell* for the Clyde instead of trying to make it back to Liverpool, for if fog held them out of Liverpool, as he knew from hard experience it could, they would find themselves in dire straits as the food ran out.

Bluebell responded to the call made on her and sped safely homewards, hour by hour making good passage through still fretful seas. It was blowing a sou-wester as she entered the Firth of Clyde on Sunday, October 20, with some of the masters bent to the task of making out a rough list of the survivors from their ships. At midday, Chief Officer Coultas of *Scoresby* left the bridge and went down into the wardroom to eat. His ration for that meal was a piece of corned beef about one and a half inches square, together with the crumbs at the bottom of a biscuit tin. *Bluebell* was literally down to her last bean.

As the corvette went up to the first buoy of the swept channel she sighted *Fowey*, who signalled her to follow in astern.

At Gourock pier that evening the weary, bedraggled survivors shuffled ashore from the two escort vessels. It was 6 p.m. when *Fowey* landed her survivors, more than a hundred and fifty of them, but if it was an emotional sight to see them pouring from the ship in the half-dark, the scene when *Bluebell* began to discharge was scarcely believable.

Commander Sherwood had no real idea how many men he had aboard until the flow started. As the number rose above two hundred and kept on rising, he exclaimed to the astonished naval officer receiving them, 'Good God, they must be coming up through a hole in the bottom - there was never enough room for all that lot!'

But the ship herself bore testimony enough to the huge number of men she had carried. Inside, all was a shambles. In the men's quarters nearly all the bunks, held by chains, were broken from the weight of exhausted men trying to sit and lie on them.

The survivors from the two ships, more than four hundred of them, waited to be officially checked in by the immigration authorities. They were grateful for cups of tea, sandwiches and cigarettes handed out to them by the WVS and the Church Army. They were questioned by newspaper reporters, but cautioned by officers and masters not to give away any information.

'Aw, come on lads,' pleaded the reporters. 'All the stories will be killed by the censor anyway . . .'

They were packed into a large hall for a meal, it seemed

crowded to the roof. Afterwards, sections of them split up and went their separate ways, the seamen to be looked after by the British Sailors' Society and the WVS, the officers to hotel accommodation somehow found for them.

The officers from *Empire Miniver* were taken to a hotel so full that they had to bed down on mattresses placed on the floor of the lounge. But at least they were able to sleep between sheets for the first time since the attack on SC7 began. Those from the *Sheka-tika* went to a hotel where unbelievably they were not allowed into the dinning-room because they were not properly dressed; most of them were in uniform, but with no collar and tie, only a heavy jersey, and wearing seaboots, just as they had gone to their lifeboats. However, they were allowed to go up to their bedrooms and eat there. To add a little cheer to the occasion they managed to buy a bottle of whisky between them by whipping together what cash they had.

In the morning they signed off at the shipping office and went on survivor's leave; they and hundreds of others, almost un-noticed now. The reporters were right, of course; there wasn't a word about in in the newspapers, nor would there ever be.

Bluebell and *Fowey*, after taking aboard some emergency rations, went on to Liverpool. There was another convoy to take out, another convoy to bring in.

But *Bluebell* still carried one survivor, the German Shepherd dog which young Sture Mattsson had saved from the sinking *Gunborg*. The kindly sailors had warned the boy that if he took his pet ashore it would have to go into quarantine. Sadly, there-fore, he had given the animal a last hug and left it in the safe hands of the corvette's crew.

11

How Do You Feel, Captain?

'October 21, Monday. 8.30 a.m. Berthed alongside Prince's Pier and disembarked survivors.'

So ran *Leith*'s brief report. All the survivors were up on deck as she came alongside at Liverpool at that cold hour in the morning. There were more than a hundred of them, officers and men from the *Assyrian*, *Empire Brigade*, *Soesterberg* and *Nora*, the Estonian ship whose crew she had picked up from their rafts before SC7's nightmare began.

There to greet them all were a small crowd of dockyard workers, two WVS tea trolleys, a few naval officers, some waiting transport lorries, an ambulance and doctor.

They came ashore wearing a weird assortment of clothing; the lucky ones, that is. Others were half naked, clutching blankets around them. There was no rank visible among the rescued. Captain de Jong, the little master of *Soesterberg*, whose survivors had lost their boots, shoes and socks in the leaking lifeboat, now wore shoes several sizes too big for him which he had scrounged from an ox of an engineer. The old shoes had cracked heels, and the Dutch master shuffled along in them feeling, as he put it, like a Chinese with his first pair of shoes who did not know whether to put his feet or his hands in them. This in addition to a black face, a three-day beard and no cap.

As the survivors walked and limped along the landing stage they passed the stewards of a Cunarder loading meat.

'Which ship?' the loaders called.

'Dozens,' came the laconic reply.

The Cunarder men nearly dropped their load.

It was a grey scene on this early morning, but as always there was a joker to relieve the gloom. He was a rescued seaman aged nearly seventy, married with eight or nine children at home, who had not been able to keep still aboard *Leith*, always busying himself sweeping up and cleaning the messdecks, jawing with the ship's company and telling them how much he longed to get back on the nest. He was an irrepressible character who won the hearts of everyone aboard, and got a big cheer as he walked down the gangway.

Then soon all were gone, many to the Seamen's Mission, where some men in tatters, like *Assyrian*'s Radio Officer Stracy and Second Mate Frank Bellas, were served out with Weaver To Wearer suits, plimsolls, and old tweed caps.

The ambulance still waited on the quay. It had come for the sick Commodore. But now two women boarded the sloop.

Commodore Lachlan MacKinnon had recovered consciousness and was weakly dictating a telegram to his wife to tell her that he was still alive when, to his astonishment, she walked into his cabin with their daughter, Ione. They had learned of his critical condition aboard a warship after rescue, and had made the slow and awkward train journey up from their home at Frampton, Dorset, to meet the ship; though it was only by a mixture of good fortune and sympathetic help that they had arrived at the correct port. It was Commander Ughtred James, husband of the Commodore's other daughter in America, who, in his post in the Admiralty, had found out that his father-in-law had been picked up out of the sea seriously ill and the rescue ship was expected to arrive at a 'north-western port' within forty-eight hours. Meeting Mrs MacKinnon and her daughter from the West Country train, which was terminated outside London in order to escape the bombing, he drove them to Euston to find two expresses drawn up on opposite sides of the same platform; one bound for Liverpool and the other for Glasgow. Which one should they take? He phoned the duty officer in the Admiralty operations room.

'Liverpool is nearer than Glasgow,' came the reply. 'I should take a chance on the former . . .' And so here they were, aboard the sloop. Such were the tensions and dramas of Service families.

The Commodore was still gravely ill. By rights, once pneumonia had set in he should have died within hours, and only the 'M and B' tablets had saved him. Now Surgeon-Lieutenant Robertson refused to allow his patient to be moved from the ship until a pneumonia specialist had been sent from hospital to examine him.

Leith went upstream alongside an oiler to refuel, but no sooner had she connected up than there came a signal ordering her to return forthwith to await the arrival of the specialist. As the very motion of the ship was painful to the Commodore, who had at last found peaceful sleep, Commander Allen signalled back respectfully suggesting that he should continue oiling and return later, as per schedule.

Now Commander Dickinson of *Scarborough* came aboard. SC7's ocean escort had finally arrived at Liverpool after sighting only one lone ship from her once proud convoy; the *Somersby*, heading valiantly for the Clyde. The two escort captains now talked over the unprecedented attack on the convoy.

Another signal was received. *Leith* must return *forthwith*. The specialist had arrived at the quay to find her gone, and he was angry as he left; the senior officer in command of escorts was angry; and the surgeon captain who now met the sloop as she returned to the jetty after oiling up was very, very angry. Bleary-eyed, brusque and impatient, he looked in on the Commodore for one minute, then called out 'Bring in the stretcher!'

The young ship's doctor tried to argue his point that a specialist should examine the Commodore first, but his protests were waved away by the senior man, who also answered the inquiries of the anxious relatives with the merest strained politeness. White faced, Surgeon-Lieutenant Robertson accompanied his patient to the hospital. He had pulled the admiral through so far, and would not leave him now until he knew he was in expert hands.

The abrupt departure of the Commodore dashed the hopes among those of *Leith*'s crew who thought that his inability to be moved would bring them a welcome respite in dock. Instead, *Leith* now moved to her usual berth at Gladstone Dock, the lower deck was cleared and the ship's company mustered on the jetty in an open warehouse to face a forbidding array of top brass. There was the First Lord of the Admiralty, Mr. A. V. Alexander, and other Cabinet Ministers, together with the immaculately dressed Admiral Sir Percy Noble, Commander-in-Chief, Western Approaches, and a number of flag officers. Admiral Noble delivered a 'pep talk' which was hardly music on the ears. As bad a time as they had been through so far, he warned, it was only a taste of what was to come during the following year . . .

But after the bad news, the good. They were to have a few days' leave.

Home!

Home to wives and girl friends. To a flutter on the Unity football pools. To a visit to the pictures: Mickey Rooney in an Andy Hardy film, or Gordon Harker in 'Saloon Bar'. And to the news that men aged thirty-five were to register for military service. . . .

Home, too, for the survivors brought in by *Leith*. Some, like Second Engineer Bill Venables, had not far to go; he lived only across the city in Liverpool.

When he arrived unexpectedly at home his surprised mother said 'What's happened, Bill?'

'Oh, nothing,' he said. 'I've just got some leave.'

Then suddenly he burst into tears and told her that *Assyrian* had gone.

That's how it was. Your feelings on losing a ship in which you had spent seven years of your life were something that could not be explained; but nor could they be bottled up.

Radio Officer Robert Stracy, a man normally most particular about his uniform and appearance, arrived at his home in Manchester in his Weaver To Wearer suit, cloth cap and plimsolls, carrying his few personal belongings wrapped in a newspaper parcel.

'What on earth's the matter?' asked his wife. 'You look a wreck.'

'I've been torpedoed, love.'

Stracy's legs were swollen with a mild dose of 'immersion feet', and he would have to sleep in flannel trousers, or with his legs wrapped up in cloth, for a few days, until the trouble passed off . . .

For the rescued merchant captains as they left *Leith*, there followed the usual questioning at naval headquarters. How had the U-boat attack come about? What was their opinion of it? Were their secret papers saved or destroyed - or could they be still floating?

When the questioning was done, black-faced Captain de Jong shuffled his way through the streets of Liverpool in his oversize shoes, many times having to ask the way to the Dutch Consul. But once there, the wheels began to grind. He was given money to buy necessities for his crew, all of whom had been found accommodation, the injured being taken to hospital.

Captain de Jong sent his chief officer shopping for the men's needs. For himself, being found a room at a hotel, there followed the luxuries of a shave, a bath, a new suit, and some shoes to fit his long suffering feet. Then early to bed, to give himself a 'good farmer's night'. He wrote about that night afterwards, in expressive terms.

'The Hun did not grant me this, however, because as soon as I was sleeping peacefully the first German bombers arrived about ten o'clock over Liverpool, and gave the town the full treatment. It was raining bombs, and behind the hotel stood a large ack-ack gun. When this went into action it shook the whole hotel to its foundations. It was as if you were in a ballast ship in bad weather, when you lie in your bunk and are flung from one side to the other, when the ship comes with its head out of water and then returns with a smack down to the sea, and everything starts creaking and groaning. It was the same feeling here when a bomb landed in the immediate neighbourhood. One explosion followed after the other.

'I thought, "You dirty Hun, you can do what you can but you will have to throw me out of bed because I am too tired." Luckily the raid finished at midnight, and the Germans flew off, leaving behind them a burning town with big rubble heaps. The electric light had gone out, apparently the powerhouse had been hit, and many streets had no water nor gas. A lot of houses were hit round about us, but the hotel fortunately was saved.

'In the morning there were many buildings still burning. When on my way to the office of the Netherlands Shipping Company I met our Dutch Consul, who was looking for another office because his own building had been hit. This is how it went on for a number of nights in Liverpool, and large parts of the city were destroyed. Nevertheless, through all this the people stayed calm. They took it as it came, without grumbling, believing in victory in the end.'

Meanwhile the surviving ships of SC7 had all successfully found their way to the Clyde, either during the same Sunday night that saw the arrival of *Bluebell* and *Fowey*, or the day after.

The *Botusk*, after nearly going aground on the Irish coast, found a warship that escorted her as far as Stranraer. In thick weather later *Botusk* unwittingly steamed straight over a British minefield, but she got safely through to arrive at Gourock the day after *Fowey*.

The aged *Dioni* steamed in, lone survivor of the four Greeks. So did the *Valparaiso*, the only surviving Swede. Fog, a deep, rolling fog, had been Captain Oscar Asplund's good friend.

Then there were five Norwegians: *Karlander*, *Inger Elisabeth*, *Havorn*, *Sneland 1*, and the ancient tanker, the *Thoroy*. Torpedoes had narrowly missed her old plates, but she had thumped on. Born 1893, still going strong.

There was the Danish *Flynderborg*, and the scruffy old British tramp, *Trident*. She had narrowly escaped two torpedoes which crossed her path - God bless her for being so slow! When *Trident* reached Barry Docks later, a generous shipping company would give each of her crew a bonus of £5 and three days' leave, and the officers £10 extra on their wages.

Like *Trident*, the old Hull ship *Corinthic* arrived at anchor during the Sunday night. It rained all that night, and next day there was a heavy mist, but keen eyes looked anxiously for the shapes of familiar vessels, and were relieved to find some of them.

Corinthic moved off first from anchorage, and the crews of each ship came on deck and waved their caps as she passed.

'How do you feel this morning, captain?' sang out *Somersby*'s Captain Bill Thompson.

'Better than I did on Friday night!' answered fiery little Captain George Nesbitt.

'Good luck . . .' the cry came back through the mist.

Was this all, then - the remains of a thirty-five ship convoy? No, there was one more.

To great cheers, the damaged *Carsbreck* came limping in, shepherded by the faithful *Heartsease*. It was a remarkable achievement by the Glasgow steamer; holed and head down, she went gratefully to anchor.

Heartsease did not stop her engines. Just in to deliver her charge, then straight out again and on to Liverpool. She now carried nine survivors which she had picked up while escorting *Carsbreck*; the men had been adrift in a lifeboat for a day and a half when she spotted them.

Outside Liverpool, 'Heart Disease' had to anchor when she ran into thick fog; the same troublesome fog that had decided *Bluebell*'s Commander Sherwood against taking his crowded ship there. No matter, all the time they were anchored counted towards their next boiler-clean, with its reward of leave.

As the corvette waited for the fog to lift, Commander North, the countryman, took an apple from the box of good Oxfordshire Cox's sent to him by his parents and began a letter to them.

'We shall soon be back in port again after another trip which has lasted a bit longer than usual owing to us having some more incidents . . . This time we had it very fine and it was quite smooth except for one night when it was blowing and raining . . . During our trips we generally have various kinds of birds round the ship. This time we had several starlings, I don't know where they came from. . . .'

You couldn't tell much of the real thing to a family, even should you be allowed to do so. No more than you could give a suitable answer to visitors like the Cabinet Minister he had recently been obliged to show round the ship.

'Well, Commander, I must say you all look *very* comfortable . . .'

All accounted for, but not quite. There were still more survivors to come in from the cheated Atlantic. And, surprisingly, one more ship.

Back in the disaster area as daylight broke after the night attack, the second lifeboat from *Blairspey*, thankfully intact after narrowly escaping the third torpedo to hit the ship, found itself alone on a freshening sea. Then a vessel was sighted on the horizon. Incredibly it was the *Blairspey*. The big Glasgow ship had drifted some thirty miles south since being hit, and in spite of the heavy damage from the three torpedoes was still afloat on her cargo of timber.

As they gazed at her unbelievingly from a distance, a Sunderland from Coastal Command broke out of the clouds and began to circle the derelict. They yelled and waved, but the flying boat did not see them. After inspecting the ship it flew off.

Later they found they had company on this desolate morning, when another lifeboat came into sight. In it were the survivors of *Sedgepool*. These men, too, had sighted a ship soon after dawn. It turned out to be . . . *Sedgepool*. With their captain and others lost, they were debating whether to pull across to the badly damaged hulk and climb aboard her to get some dry clothes, when the big vessel suddenly nosed into the water, her stern came up, and she disappeared downwards with the cargo of grain she had been carrying to Manchester. Jokingly they had said earlier in the voyage that it was the only convoy the old *Sedgepool* had ever managed to keep up with. Her first, and her last.

Now the two lifeboats hailed each other and discussed what they should do. The *Sedgepool* boat decided to carry on and try to make the long voyage to the Butt of Lewis, but the *Blairspey* men chose to stay in sight of the derelict, as they felt sure that the Sunderland would have reported her and that a ship would be sent to investigate.

In fact help did come, but from an unexpected quarter. The ocean tug *Salvonia* had sailed out from Campbeltown in answer to the distress messages sent out by *Shekatika*. When she arrived the *Shekatika* had gone, but she then came upon *Blairspey?*

At 5 p.m. in a tossing sea, the fourteen weary occupants of the lifeboat saw the tug appear alongside the ship. The excited waving began again, and this time, thank heaven, they were seen. The tug closed in, and there began the difficult and dangerous business of transferring from the lifeboat to her in the now very high seas. But an hour later all were safely aboard.

Salvonia's shrewd captain was convinced that in spite of the great damage done to her, there was an even chance of the *Blairspey* remaining afloat, and he decided to take her in tow. But in the growing darkness and angry sea it was impossible to connect up. *Salvonia*, it was clear, would have to wait for daylight and a break in the rough weather conditions before she could begin work. As there was also the danger of a U-boat still prowling in the area the tug withdrew at high speed, zigzagging as she went, to pass the night at a safe and wary distance from the derelict.

At dawn the following morning – Sunday, October 20 – *Salvonia* returned and, in more favourable weather and seas, made fast the tow. But not only did she salve an empty hulk, her timely reappearance in the area that day also brought rescue for the *Sedgepool* lifeboat, which in the night's heavy seas had not made much distance, and for one of the two boats from *Clintonia*, under Chief Officer Buglass. When she had got all the newcomers safely aboard the 500-ton tug carried survivors from three vessels . . . and still her work was far from finished.

All through Sunday the *Salvonia* towed the reeling, lurching *Blairspey*, and next day she picked up yet more survivors, in one lifeboat but from two ships. They were officers and men from the steamers *Port Gisborne* and *St Malo*, which had been sunk much earlier on an HX convoy from Halifax. The survivors had spent ten grim days in their boat.

The tug now had more than a hundred grateful survivors on board. One of them was Chief Engineer James Aves of *Sedgepool*. In his pocket was a photograph of his family, practically the only possession he was left with. It had got very tattered while he was swimming after jumping from his abandoned ship, but had dried out quite well. Now, in the warmth of rescue, he got some of his fellow survivors, and members of the crew of *Salvonia*, to autograph the back of it; it became possibly the only personal record of their common drama.

For four more days and nights *Salvonia* hauled the drunken *Blairspey* through the dangerous waters of the Western Approaches, and on Friday, October 25, seven days after surviving the explosions of the three German torpedoes, the battered steamer was towed into the Clyde. When she was put to anchor, some idea of the blast she had suffered could be had from the sight of the engineers' accommodation sticking weirdly six feet out from her side.

Like *Carsbreck*, the other damaged Glasgow steamer which had limped in a few days before her, the *Blairspey* drew some resounding cheers.

There only remained the second lifeboat of survivors from the *Clintonia*. This, under Captain Irvin, had hoisted sail at daybreak to attempt the long journey home, but during the morning they were luckily spotted by the same Sunderland which had circled the derelict *Blairspey*. The sea was far too rough for the flying boat to come down on the water so it dropped them a bag full of food, together with a chart of their position, and a note from the pilot promising to send help.

After the plane flew off they continued slowly on course, scanning the empty sea for hour after dreary hour for any sign of a rescuer. Then, just as the evening dark was gathering on a rising sea, a searching British destroyer came fast over the horizon towards them. They were taken safely aboard and eventually landed at Londonderry.

When, days later, Captain Irvin finally reported to his shipping office on Tyneside, there was one last painful task for him to perform. The member of the crew who, during *Clintonia*'s violent night, had been fatally hurled into the breech of the ship's gun, and later cast to the sea from the lifeboat, had lived just across the river from the office, and the captain was asked to visit the man's sister and break the bad news gently to her.

Such could be the unenviable duties of a master.

The same woman's young son had been *Clintonia*'s cabin boy. As Captain Irvin walked to pay his sad call, he could only thank God that the lad had been spared and he was not having to carry the news of a double tragedy.

12

The Second Assault

The brilliantly executed action against SC7 would have been triumph enough for Admiral Doenitz's 'wolves', but the slaughter did not end there. It continued, only hours later, with huge losses being inflicted on a fast HX convoy coming up in the rear of the slow convoy. The result was a double action which produced the blackest statistics of the war at sea since hostilities had begun.

Just like SC7, the fast convoy HX79, and its unsuspecting escorts, sailed headlong into an assault by a U-boat pack. The attack took place on the night of Saturday, October 19 - the night following the assault on SC7 - about 250 miles west of the scene of SC7's destruction.

Some of the 'wolves' who had attacked SC7 took part in the new assault. Otto Kretschmer (U-99), Fritz Frauenheim (U-101) and Karl-Heinz Moehle (U-123) had all started home to base following the attack on SC7, having expended all their torpedoes, but the boats of Engelbert Endrass (U-46) and Joachim Schepke (U-100) were still primed for more action and joined in the new ambush. Heinrich Bleichrodt in U-48 also returned to the fray. Since being chased off by *Scarborough* he had sunk an outward-bound straggler and now had only one usable torpedo. But he was to make it count. . . .

Convoy HX79 had sailed from Halifax days after SC7 at a good eight to nine knots. In addition to being a faster convoy, with many oil-fired ships and tankers, it was also a bigger one, consisting of 49 vessels. It had more escorts, too. Unlike SC7, with its one small escort sloop for the journey across the Atlantic, HX79 was accompanied by two big armed merchant cruisers, one of 14,000 tons and the other of 16,000 tons, while on reaching the outer limits of the Western Approaches it was met by a veritable fighting fleet consisting of two destroyers, four corvettes, a minesweeper, and three anti-submarine trawlers. For additional protection a Dutch submarine sailed in the centre of the convoy, while one of the merchantmen, the 5,000-ton steamer *Loch Lomond*, had been designated rescue ship, to pick up survivors should any vessel be torpedoed.

But although the number of escorts was so much greater, HX79 suffered from precisely the same basic problems as SC7. The escorts from the Western Approaches arrived independently, without any knowledge of the nature of the convoy or any idea who else would be there. The escort commanders did not know each other; they had limited means of communication, especially at night, when they could only talk by dimmed morse lamp; and they had no common plan of defence. Above all they did not anticipate U-boats attacking on the surface, by night, and in strength.

It was Gunther Prien, patrolling in U-47, who spotted HX79. Prien, the daring ace with the white snorting bull on his conning-tower; the man who, soon after the start of the war, had crept into the British naval stronghold of Scapa Flow and sunk the battleship *Royal Oak*. On sighting HX79, Korrettenkapitan Prien wirelessed the news back to base, and for a second time a wolf-pack gathered and closed in. In the assault Prien, Endrass, Schepke and Bleichrodt were joined by Heinrich Liebe (U-38), the commander who had sunk the *Aenos* and crippled the *Carsbreck?*

As the five U-boats moved in on HX79 the violent pattern of events of the previous night was repeated. Another night of bewilderment, confusion and frustration for the escorts as they searched for an elusive, unseen enemy, their asdics useless against the surfaced raiders, and again the terrible question of whether to stop and pick up survivors or steam on in search of the enemy, for in the event there was far too much rescue work for one ship to handle.

Once again, lookouts on some of the merchant ships could scarcely believe their eyes as they fleetingly glimpsed the shape of a conning-tower speeding close past them in the moonlight.

Surely U-boats were *undersea* craft, not meant for racing around like motor torpedo boats? It was all so totally unreal.

On the 6,000-ton motor tanker *Sitala* astonished eyes saw a small dark shape coming up from astern, speed past only about twenty yards away on the starboard beam, unmistakably the conning-tower of a U-boat, the only part of the German visible above the agitated water. Like some great shark's fin it cut away from view. The tanker then had barely twenty minutes to live. The torpedo that hit her sent *Sitala* lurching ablaze into the night, and as her crew abandoned her she was well on fire.

The dismal story of this second night's events is reflected in the experience of one ship, the newest in the convoy, and her crew. The motorship *Wandby*, from Sunderland, was returning from British Columbia on the second leg of her maiden voyage. A splendid looking ship of nearly 5,000 tons, she was in fact the last vessel built on the River Wear to pre-war standards.

Wandby carried a cargo of 1,500 tons of pig-iron and a huge load of timber rising ten or twelve feet high on her decks. She had loaded at Vancouver, sailed down the west coast of America, through the Panama Canal to Bermuda, and there joined a small convoy with instructions to join up with HX79 sailing from Halifax. This they had done, and *Wandby*'s fate was sealed . . .

The attack on HX79 came just sixteen hours after the last unfortunate ship of SC7 was sent beneath the waves. It was still the same day - October 19 - though darkness had fallen once again, as the new pack closed in.

At 9 p.m. *Wandby*'s Captain John Kenny saw a sudden glare six miles away on the starboard quarter. It was the explosion from the first ship to be torpedoed, which sank quickly with her captain and a third of her crew.

During the next two hours, as HX79 steamed on under the revealing light of a misty moon, three more ships were sunk. Then it was *Wandby*'s turn.

At about 10.30 p.m. a torpedo struck *Wandby* just forward of the engine-room on the port side, causing a tremendous explosion which blew away the ship's port lifeboat and hurled the ship's fifty-year-old master six feet into the air from where he stood on the port side of the bridge, injuring his leg as he fell. Everyone else escaped either bruised or shaken, but the ship which, only weeks ago, Captain Kenny had stood by as she was proudly completed, had been fatally hit. Her side was leaking badly - she had already started to break up - and the fuel pipe to the donkey boiler was fractured beyond repair. As her auxiliaries were steam driven, the loss of the boiler left them without the use of pumps, steering engine and dynamo, and the ship at the mercy of the incoming sea. Though *Wandby* might float for some time, supported by her timber cargo, her crew could not do a thing to save her.

Captain Kenny ordered abandon ship, and they clambered, all thirty-five of them, into the one remaining lifeboat, the master being the last to leave. They went in orderly fashion, and, due to the master's foresight, prepared as best they could for a long sojourn in the boat. He ensured that each officer was handed a bottle of scotch or brandy, with orders not to open it until instructed to do so, and that tins of cigarettes were distributed among the crew. There was no knowing how long the boat would have to be their refuge.

After two hours, however, the armed trawler HMS *Angle* hove into sight, and eventually closed the boat to take them aboard; 'Angel' they gratefully renamed her later. It was as they were being picked up by *Angle* that the full horror of the night, and the fortunate circumstances of their own escape, was brought home to them.

There was a muffled explosion, and at the same time all the air around them seemed to be sucked away, leaving them in a vacuum. Then, five miles away to the west, a ball of flame erupted to the night sky and a ship's superstructure could be seen passing through the flames high into the air. The sea was ablaze for miles around. So bright was the sky and sea that when Captain Kenny's small case containing his ship's secret papers was accidentally dropped and floated far away from the trawler's side, it was easily spotted and retrieved from the sea by the trawler's boat.

All the men of *Wandby* could think of at their moment of rescue was the appalling way in which the crew of that exploding petrol tanker must have died.

The subsequent events of the night were like the continuation of a bad dream. More explosions, distress calls, and baffled escorts steaming in circles, unable to find the enemy.

Daybreak found *Angle* steaming through a weird sea of sinking ships and half-ships and patches of burning oil, searching for other survivors but finding none. Then into sight came the derelict *Wandby*, still afloat, and she was boarded; but it was found that the engine-room was flooded to the tops of the main engines and she was breaking up fast. The boarding party returned to the trawler and *Angle* continued her search for survivors among the floating wreckage from other ships, but there was no sign of life anywhere. When she swept round again on the completion of her mercy patrol *Wandby* had gone. So had every other derelict but one, an 8,000-ton motor tanker, the *Caprella*. She had been torpedoed for'ard of the bridge, and although her bow was very low in the water she did not appear to be sinking any deeper. When a party climbed aboard to inspect the damage there seemed to be a fair prospect of bringing her in. After all that lost shipping - salvage!

A 'crew' consisting of *Wandby*'s chief engineer, senior third engineer and carpenter, together with eight ratings from *Angle*, including a signalman, now boarded *Caprella* and got to work. The ship's donkey boiler was still warm, and after half an hour on the hand-pump the two engineers had raised enough steam to start the oil-burning equipment. Slowly the Shell tanker began to move off, astern of the trawler.

The approach of darkness, however, brought a turn in the weather, the wind freshened from the east and raised a head-swell which caused the tanker to pitch ominously - and at four a.m. she began to break up. The boarding party, now all gathered aft, could see the foc'sle head rising and falling between the lower and upper bridge for all the world as if the for'ard section was attached to the rest of the vessel by huge hinges. Then the bizarre moment came when the for'ard section broke away. As it sank, the jumper stay between the two masts did not part until it had forced the top part of the mainmast to a crazy angle, and when it did finally part it was like a shot from a four-inch gun.

Now the boarding party were marooned on the still floating half-ship with no means of abandoning it. They sent up a distress flare. *Angle* steamed back to the rescue, but when her boat was launched it sank to the gunwales; excessive use had made it unseaworthy. All that was left now was a Carley raft. *Angle* attempted to fire a line by rifle on the leeward side of the half-ship, so that the boarders could pull the raft across to them. But the wind had risen and this plan proved abortive; the trawler had to steam in circles and could only fire each time she passed.

Angle's coxswain, a deepsea fisherman, now gave the finest display of ship-handling any man there had witnessed, as he brought the trawler round in the heavy swell dangerously close under the tanker's stern, so that a line could be thrown over to her deck. It was caught amid a shower of fruity language.

But the men were not out of danger yet. The first party to take to the raft in the dark found themselves unable to paddle it away from the tanker, the angry sea nearly washing them into the torn portion of one of the hulk's mid-ship tanks. *Angle* came in close again and passed over another heaving line; they now had a line from the raft to the trawler as well as one back to the tanker; and with one line being heaved on and the other paid out, they were able to get alongside *Angle* and board her, then send the raft back for the remaining men.

Even in these seas the derelict half-ship still remained afloat, apparently the only remaining evidence of the U-boat pack's attack on the convoy. It was a danger to shipping; *Angle* sank the hulk with four shells from her four-inch gun.

Gone were all the hopes of salvage. Gone, too, along with *Wandby* and *Caprella*, were ten other ships of HX79, as they would discover later. The last ship of the convoy to be sunk was the steamer *Loch Lomond* - the designated rescue ship - whose crew themselves, together with survivors they had picked up, had to be rescued by the escort minesweeper. Yet another ship, a big tanker, was damaged but managed to limp into port.

And even then the immediate slaughter by the U-boats was not over. During the same night, an outward-bound convoy also ran foul of surfaced raiders at a cost of seven more merchantmen. All this without loss to Doenitz's 'wolves', who returned jubilantly to base to be greeted by eager war correspondents and photographers. It was a homecoming of heroes.

Official records credited Otto Kretschmet (U-99) with sinking seven ships during the night attack on SC7 - hearly half the night's total losses. Karl-Heinz Moehle (U-123) sank four ships, and the remainder were shared between Engelbert Endrass (U-46), Joachim Schepke (U-100) and Fritz Frauenheim (U-101) - it was he who sank the *Assyrian*. Endrass and Schepke enhanced their scores by sinking another three ships each of HX79.

It was a time for medals, justly won and quickly awarded, for Admiral Doenitz believed that none of his commanders should have to wait long for his honours.

One man only on the other side received a medal; for which, in the British order of things, he had to wait. Captain Reginald Sanderson Kearon of the *Assyrian* was awarded the OBE, a tribute to his ship and his men as well as to his own personal courage. His inspiring conduct that night, culminating in his effort to save the life of his elderly chief officer, also brought him another award, that of the Lloyd's War Medal For Bravery At Sea. The medal, with its distinctive blue and silver ribbon, was bestowed upon officers and men of the Merchant Navy and fishing fleets in cases of exceptional gallantry at sea.

And so there it was. The final miserable statistics for the month of October, 1940, recorded the highest tonnage sunk by U-boats since the war began; a total of 352,407 tons. In more human terms this meant the loss of sixty-three merchant ships, almost a third of these from one convoy, SC7. It was the peak achievement of the four-month period, July to October, 1940, which the U-boat commanders called 'the happy time.'

These figures were only disclosed long afterwards. How close to the truth the German claims at the time came, may be seen from this communique issued by the German High Command on October 20, 1940:

'On the night of October 19th German submarines sank 17 merchant ships with a total tonnage of 110,000 in a British convoy. Other submarines report the sinking of 43,000 tons from other convoys. Thus within two days, by the destruction of two convoys and by single successes, 327,000 tons of enemy merchant shipping has been sunk.'

This enemy communique was, understandably, given little mention in Britain.

So SC7 slipped into naval history as a disaster to be bleakly remembered, its story one of inadequacy, unpreparedness and grim endurance on the part of the British, and cool, rewarding enterprise by the Germans in launching their first big night swoop by a wolf-pack. The enemy had evolved his new style of U-boat warfare by building on the hard lessons learned in the last war; yet, looking at the British state of unpreparedness, it seemed almost as if for the Royal Navy that war had never happened. All the naval escorts of SC7 had been built after the lessons of 1914-18 might have been amply digested, yet their limitations were painfully obvious. And, ostrich-like, secure in its possession of the asdic underwater detector, the Navy had not seemed to realize how naked it was against an enemy submarine operating on the surface. The enemy's surface speed had also been greatly underestimated.

By his own admission, no one was more surprised than Admiral Doenitz himself at the very completeness of the success of his first major assault by night surfaced U-boats operating in unison; he could not believe that the British had not foreseen this eventuality, especially with the knowledge of successes gained by night surfaced U-boats in the latter stages of World War I.

Yet even after the devastating attack on SC7 it was some time before the threat posed by U-boats working together was fully grasped by the British naval command. All Commander Allen of *Leith*, the senior escort of SC7, could report was that he judged at least three U-boats to have taken part in the attack; but he could, and did, stress most strongly the need for better communication between escorts, and for teamwork against attack.

It was all to come. The formation of regular escort groups, skilled at working together. Better communications, with radio-telephony installed in warships. Direction-finding radio, which could quickly locate a talkative U-boat. The 'snowflake' rocket, which lit up the night sky far brighter than starshell, and was free of its flashback and other handicaps. The provision of medically-manned convoy rescue ships. And, most important of all, the installation of ship's radar, to give immediate warning of a surfaced enemy.

Few of the U-boat 'aces' of 1940 would see these changes. Within a year, three of the five 'wolves' who attacked SC7 would be lost; Schepke and Endrass, both killed in action, and Otto Kretschmer, taken prisoner after his boat was sunk.

But that was tomorrow.

13

Last Ship to Die

How do you thank someone for saving your life? It was a question that came up all too often for seamen on the North Atlantic run but you did your best, as did the survivors of SC7 who later wrote to thank the escorts who had brought them home out of the sea.

Some went further, and one letter that found its way to *Bluebell* took Commander Sherwood and his ship's company 'flat-aback'. It was a thank you letter from Captain Wilfred Brett of the sunken *Beatus*, enclosing a cheque for £7, the proceeds of a 'whip-round' among his grateful crew. The merchant men's generous token of their appreciation was put into *Bluebell*'s kitty.

For most of the survivors of SC7, after a few days' leave, it was a case of another ship and another convoy. And so their war would continue from one voyage to the next, and for some, from one lost ship to another.

Some men would not survive a second time. Like Radio Officer Robert Stracy of *Assyrian*. In 1944 his ship was one of four merchant vessels which missed a convoy and had to sail on together in the Indian Ocean, unescorted. Japanese submarines attacked the four ships and sank them all; there were no survivors. And Second Mate Ort, the patient, resourceful officer who so greatly helped the captain of the *Soesterberg*. He volunteered for special duties and was parachuted into Holland as a radio

…ator for 'Radio England', but was taken prisoner and later …ecuted by the Germans.

Most of the surviving ships of SC7 were quickly to vanish. Of the seven British vessels which got away, only two of them were left after another year of war.

The old *Botusk*, the ship with the unlovely name given to her by the Board of Trade when rescued from the scrapheap, sank miserably only three months after SC7, when she struck a mine off the coast of Inverness-shire. At the time, the Commodore of the convoy believed it to be a U-boat attack; two other ships were lost, the remainder of the convoy cracking on at full speed. *Botusk* sank in two minutes with the loss of two men, her survivors being picked up hours later by a Post Office cable ship. It then transpired that the convoy had run into a British minefield. . . .

The Hull scrap carrier *Corinthic*, raised from underwater to fight her war, returned underwater to a deeper grave on April 13, 1941, when torpedoed off the coast of West Africa.

Somersby, the big 5,000-ton Tynesider whose brief glory it had been to lead the remnants of SC7, was torpedoed and sunk on May 13, 1941 at 26 degrees West in the North Atlantic, far west of the SC7 graveyard. All her crew were rescued by a Greek ship.

Trident, the scruffy Tynesider as old as the Kaiser's war, never did fall victim to a torpedo. She died at a buoy off the Tyne on August 2, 1941, when bombed and sunk by enemy aircraft. All her crew, too, got clear.

The damaged *Carsbreck* was repaired and sailed successfully on other convoys until, in October, 1941, almost a year to the day when she limped into the Clyde, a U-boat found her. She was torpedoed and sunk off southern Spain, on the Gibraltar run, with heavy loss of life.

As fate would have it, it was the other, more heavily damaged ship of the convoy, the *Blairspey*, which came through the war. The damage from three torpedoes was so great that she had to be halved amidships and a new forward section built, after which she put to sea again as the *Empire Spey*. At war's end she reverted again to the name of *Blairspey* and went back to her peacetime calling.

The only other British ship of SC7 to survive the war was the redoubtable Laker, *Eaglescliffe Hall*. During her wartime work around Britain's coasts she was 'Mentioned in Despatches' when, on being attacked by enemy aircraft, her crew removed a bomb from the stokehold before it exploded. Two men lost their lives during that attack. After the war *Eaglescliffe Hall* took a fair weather passage back to Canada and resumed her 'sweet water' trade.

Among SC7's eight surviving foreigners the luckiest of all was, surprisingly, the ancient Norwegian tanker *Thoroy*, the oldest ship of the convoy. The ex-British vessel, built in 1893, steamed on unscathed through the war as she had the one before, and in 1947, at the venerable age of fifty-four, was sold to the Turks.

But others of the foreign ships were by no means as fortunate. The first to go, in particularly distressing circumstances, was the Swedish motor vessel *Valparaiso?* Only two months after surviving SC7, having in the meantime recrossed to Canada, she left Halifax on December 18 with a fast HX convoy. When at 23 degrees West, about 250 miles south of Iceland, the convoy separated in fog and bad weather. *Valparaiso* disappeared with her crew of thirty-three and was never seen or heard of again. She was one of 254 ships (and 1,400 seamen) lost by Sweden in the war.

The Greek *Dioni* went aground in Milford Haven and was subsequently lost. The Danish *Flynderborg* was torpedoed and sunk by a U-boat off Newfoundland in November, 1941. Hardly a year later, in September, 1942, another U-boat torpedoed and sank the Norwegian *Inger Elisabeth* in the Gulf of St Lawrence.

But the most tragic fate of all was that which befell the Norwegian *Sneland 1*, the little barnacled tramp that had only caught SC7 by the skin of her teeth. Her end came in the dying hours of the war.

It was May 7, 1945. Germany's unconditional surrender had been signed by General Jodl and orders to cease-fire had been given. Up in the Firth of Forth that night, as both merchant ships and warships celebrated by burning flares, firing rockets and exchanging congratulatory messages, *Sneland 1* was one of a number of ships from whom it was duty as usual as they steamed out to form the familiar north-bound convoy. She was captained still by Captain Laegland, as she had been on SC7.

On the convoy this night, for the first time since the war began, the men off-watch would undress to enjoy a peaceful sleep in their bunks; for although the official end to hostilities in Europe was still twenty-four hours away, everyone felt that it was as good as over already.

But for one still active U-boat it was not. At three minutes past 11 p.m. Kapitanleutnant Klusmeier, commander of U-2336, fired his first torpedo. Thirty-five seconds later *Sneland 1* rocked with the explosion. Then another torpedo struck the British *Avondale Park.*

Both ships sank quickly. Aboard *Sneland 1*, Captain Laegland and everyone on the bridge was killed; seven in all lost their lives.

All those years, all those hazardous miles, for this.

The two ships were the last victims of a German U-boat in the Second World War.

SC7's naval escort commanders went on to see the tide turn against the wolf-packs, and indeed the whole of the sea war swing against the enemy.

Commander Dickinson of *Scarborough* gained the DSO, in addition to his DSC, as Captain Dickinson, RN, for bravery and skill in the operations in which the Allied forces were landed in North Africa; afterwards he took command of the aircraft carrier HMS *Victorious.* Lieutenant-Commander North of *Heartsease* progressed to take command of the aircraft carrier HMS *Activity*, as Captain North, RNR.

After *Leith*, Commander Allen worked in the Admiralty on the planning of the landings in North Africa, and sailed with the Fleet to Algiers, where he served on General Eisenhower's staff. He later commanded the cruiser HMS *Ceres* in the Normandy landings.

Lieutenant-Commander Aubrey of *Fowey* went on to command the sloop HMS *Wren* in the highly successful 2nd Escort Group of U-boat killers led by Captain F. J. 'Johnny' Walker, RN; and afterwards, as a Commander, Aubrey became senior officer of his own escort group in the fast frigate *Exe.*

From the viewpoint of SC7, perhaps the supreme revenge came for Lieutenant-Commander Sherwood of *Bluebell.* In May, 1943, in the new frigate HMS *Tay*, Sherwood commanded the escort of convoy ONS5 in a pitched battle against a horde of converging U-boats. It proved to be the turning point in the Battle of the Atlantic. Twelve merchant ships of the convoy were lost, but the final cost to the enemy was high: one U-boat sunk or damaged for every British loss. It was a crushing defeat for the Germans.

Sherwood had seen the wheel turn full circle. Three years before, in the *Bluebell*, he had been caught helpless by the first shattering assault by a wolf-pack; now he had been instrumental in dealing a blow from which the demoralized 'wolves' would never recover.

Of SC7's five naval escort vessels, all but one came safely

through the war. That one was . . . *Bluebell*. In the months and years after SC7 she rescued many more men from the sea, and helped avenge them, too, on arduous convoy work. She tasted the rigours of the stormy Arctic run to Russia, and it was up there, on the icy rim of the world, that her luck finally ran out. Her commander at the time was the rather raw 'Number One' of SC7 days, now a well seasoned veteran - Lieutenant G. H. Walker, DSC, RNVR.

On February 17, 1945 *Bluebell* was escorting a convoy in the bleak Barents Sea. Shortly after three o'clock in the afternoon of a murky day, she was hit by a torpedo from a U-boat. She blew up and sank at once with the loss of six officers, including her commander, and about eighty ratings. Only one man survived.

14

Your Sixpences, Please

And Commodore Lachlan MacKinnon? He was out of hospital at Liverpool in three weeks. The miracle patient. Soon afterwards, from his home in Dorset, he was ready to report for his next sea duty, fit, well and anxious to get on with the job.

But there followed weeks of waiting, of puzzling, non-committal answers to his enquiries. No matter how he tried or what he did, not one seemed to want anything to do with him.

Eventually the reason for the Navy's embarrassed sidestepping was made clear. Despite his remarkable recovery, and the fact that men years older than he were on Commodore duty, he was judged to be no longer fit for sea physically. SC7 had been his last voyage.

It was a tremendous shock, but MacKinnon was equal to it.

A few months afterwards, in the early summer of 1941, the town of Dorchester held its War Weapons Week. It took a lot of planning, a lot of hard work, for money was short, and the organizers had to go to all sorts of lengths to try to attract it. Fun and games was the order of the day, anything that would cadge a penny. At the entrance to a cinema, for instance, there was a big boarded picture of Hitler sitting in a tin bath. 'Help to drown Hitler!' was the invitation, which you did by throwing pennies in the bath and raising the level of the water.

From stall to stall, giving encouragement to the helpers including his wife and daughter, and to those considering parting with their money, went the organizer of the whole thing; a silvery haired, erect man of about sixty, dressed in a tweedy sports jacket and flannel bags, smoking a pipe and stabbing the air with it occasionally to make his point. One of his best ideas was the sideshow where a toy U-boat was placed in a glass tank set up on the pavement. The customer paid sixpence and was given three marbles which he had to drop down into the water at an angle so as to hit the U-boat and sink it. The organizer was delighted to demonstrate to anyone how to do it, and as they watched him happily 'bomb' the toy in the tank they were not to know that not long ago, in night seas a mile deep, he had clung weakly to a piece of floating timber and fought to stay alive.

'There, you see, it's sunk!'

He joined the voluntary staff of the National Savings movement, speaking at war factories and savings week rallies; he travelled the country, often having to stand for hours in crowded trains despite his rank and age. His talent for the personal touch, his outspokenness and his sense of humour made him welcome everywhere. And he always turned up. You could rely on MacKinnon.

A.B.s and admirals, you did what you could. You did your bit. That's how it was.

Acknowledgments

The authors are grateful to the masters, officers and seamen of the Merchant Navy, and officers and men of the Royal Naval Reserve, Royal Naval Volunteer Reserve, and Royal Navy, whose warm-hearted response and assistance made possible this story of convoy SC7.

THE MERCHANTMEN

Clifford Atkinson of Beverley, Yorks. (Second Radio Officer, ss. *Trident*).
Raymond Baldwin of Whiteparish, Wilts. (Second Radio Officer, ss. *Shekatika*).
Captain Wilfred L. Brett of Cardiff (Master, ss. *Beatus*).
Hilton Brodie of Croftfoot, Glasgow (Chief Cook, ss. *Carsbreck*).
Captain Ronald Coultas of Ravenscar, Yorks. (Chief Officer, ss. *Scoresby*).
John R. Crawford of Wishaw, Lanarkshire (Second Radio Officer, ss. *Blairspey*).
James Daley of Blundellsands, Liverpool (Chief Steward, ss. *Assyrian*).

Captain W. Algwyn Davies of Pen-y-lan, Cardiff (Master, ss. *Botusk*).
William Arthur Dean of Crosby, Liverpool (Fourth Engineer, ss. *Assyrian*).
Captain D. de Jong of Castricum, Holland (Master, ss. *Soesterberg*).
Leonard Dewar of Handsworth, Birmingham (First Radio Officer, ss. *Empire Brigade*).
Gilbert Michael Hing of Pelsall, Saffs. (Third Mate, ss. *Empire Miniver*).
Henry Hotchkiss of Kirkintilloch, Dunbartonshire (Second Radio Officer, ss. *Somersby*).
Kenneth C. R. Howell, MBE, of Overmonnow, Monmouth (First Radio Officer, ss. *Corinthic*).
Captain Thomas H. Irvin of North Shields, Northumberland (Master, ss. *Clintonia*).
Captain Reginald A. Leach of Tonbridge, Kent (Second Mate, ss. *Empire Miniver*).
Charles P. Littleboy of Brisbane, Australia (Radio Officer, ss. *Trevisa*).
Captain Charles R. Madsen of South Shields, Co. Durham Master, ss. *Eaglescliffe Hall*).
Captain John Mathiesen of Oslo, Norway (Chief Officer, ss. *Sneland 1*).
Sture Mattsson of Stockholm, Sweden (A.B., ss. *Gunborg*).
Bjarne Mjaanes of Auklandshamn, Norway (Steward, ss. *Sneland 1*).
Bernard J. McGovern c/o Marconi Marine (First Radio Officer, ss. *Somersby*).
Inspektor Karl J. Petersen of Gothenburg, Sweden (First Engineer, mv. *Valparaiso*).
Captain Alexander Smith of Findochty, Banffshire (Second Mate, ss. *Shekatika*).
Captain Jack Reardon Smith of Cardiff (Chief Officer, ss. *Botusk*).
Captain Robert Smith of Durham (Master, ss. *Empire Miniver*).
Chief Engineer William H. Venables of Irby, Cheshire (Second Engineer, ss. *Assyrian*).
Captain John Morrison Waters of South Shields, Co. Durham (Second Mate, ss. *Empire Brigade*).
Captain Lawrence Zebedee Weatherill of Llandaff, Cardiff (Master, ss. *Scoresby*).

And from Convoy HX79:

William J. Edbrooke of Brentwood, Essex (Senior Third Engineer, mv. *Wandby*).

James Griffiths of Rusholme, Manchester (Crew member, mv. *Sitala*).

Captain John Kenny of Arklow, Eire (Master, mv. *Wandby*).

Charles Walker of Pendlebury, Manchester (Crew member, mv. *Sitala*).

The authors thank the following relatives for their generous help:

Mrs Mary E. Aves, Hartlepool, wife of Chief Engineer James E. Aves, ss. *Sedgepool*; Mrs Elizabeth Dekonski, Arklow, Eire, daughter of Captain John Kenny, mv. *Wandby*; Miss Sally Green, Belfast, sister of Chief Officer John Green, ss. *Empire Miniver*; Kevin R. Kearon and Roy T. Kearon, Arklow, Eire, brothers of Captain Reginald S. Kearon, OBE, ss. *Assyrian*; Thoralf Laegland, Haugesund, Norway, son of Captain Laegland, ss. *Sneland 1*; Mrs Constance M. Stracy, Manchester, wife of Radio Officer Robert A. Stracy, ss. *Assyrian*; Mrs J. W. Thompson, Cardiff, wife of Captain J. William Thompson, ss. *Somersby*.

The authors thank the staff of the General Register Office of Shipping and Seamen, Cardiff, for their patient assistance during three years of research; also the Public Archives of Canada, Montreal; The Marconi International Marine Company Limited, Chelmsford, Essex; and the following shipping companies:

Rich. Amlie & Co., Haugesund, Norway; Andreadis (U.K.) Ltd., London; Billnerbolagen, Gothenburg, Sweden; Cairns, Noble & Co. Ltd., Newcastle upon Tyne; Canada Steamship Lines Ltd., Montreal; Ellerman Lines Ltd., London; Wm. France, Fenwick & Co. Ltd., London; Hall Corporation (Shipping) 1969 Ltd., Montreal; Headlam & Son, Whitby; Johnsonlinjen, Stockholm; Jacob Kjobe, Bergen, Norway; Jacob Odland, Haugesund, Norway; Sir R. Ropner & Co. Ltd., Darlington; Christian Salvesen (Managers) Ltd., Leith; Sir William Reardon Smith & Sons Ltd., Cardiff; Stag Line Ltd., North Shields; Vickers Ltd., Barrow-in-Furness; Vinke & Co., Amsterdam; Witherington & Everett, Newcastle upon Tyne.

THE NAVAL ESCORTS

Commander Robert Aubrey, DSC, RN, Ringwood, Hants. (Lieutenant-Commander, HMS *Fowey*).
George S. Boyd, Epsom, Surrey (Chief Stoker, HMS *Leith*).
Lieutenant-Commander Neil K. Boyd, DSC and Bar, RD, RNR, Barton-on-Sea, Hants. (Navigating Officer, HMS *Scarborough*).
Lieutenant Patrick N. Culverwell, RNVR, Leicester (Sub-Lieutenant, HMS *Fowey*).
Rear-Admiral N. Vincent Dickinson, CB, DSO, DSC, Alresford, Hants. (Commander, HMS *Scarborough*).
Lieutenant John D. Hill, RNVR, Ipswich (Navigating Officer, HMS *Heartsease*).
William J. Jenkins, Bramhall, Cheshire (AB/TO, RNR, HMS *Scarborough*).
Eric R. Semmens, Orpington, Kent (Telegraphist, HMS *Leith*).
Captain Robert E. Sherwood, Commander, DSO, RD, RNR, Wendover, Bucks. (Lieutenant-Commander, HMS *Bluebell*).
Commander Anthony S. Tyers, DSC, RN, Aylesbury, Bucks. (Sub-Lieutenant, HMS *Leith*).

The authors thank the following relatives for their very kind assistance:

Miss Enid Allen, London, sister of Commander Roland C. Allen, RN, HMS *Leith* (later Captain Allen, RN); Mrs Ione Carver, Farnham, Surrey, and Mrs Fynvola L. James, Northwood, Middlesex, daughters, and Captain Ughtred H. R. James, CBE, RN, son-in-law, of Vice-Admiral Lachlan Donald Ian MacKinnon, CB, CVO; Miss Cora E. North, Chinnor, Oxon., sister of Lieutenant-Commander Edward J. R. North, RNR, HMS *Heartsease* (later Captain North, RD, RNR).

Also:

R. H. Howard, London (SBA, HMS *Scarborough*).
Dr B. J. Mead, Broadstone, Dorset (Lieutenant, RNVR, HMS *Scarborough*).

Charles H. A. Scott, Dorridge, Warwicks. (Signalman, HMS *Heartsease*).
Stan Stansfield, Manchester (HMS *Scarborough*).
Douglas F. Whittaker, Hereford (Leading Signalman, HMS *Fowey*).

The authors gratefully acknowledge the special contribution made by Korvettenkapitan Heinrich Bleichrodt, Knight's Cross of the Iron Cross, Knight's Cross with Oak Leaves, of Munich, W. Germany (Kapitanleutnant, U-48); and the help of Captain K. T. Raeder, FGN, Naval Attaché, Embassy of the Federal Republic of Germany, London; and Podzun-Verlag, Bad Nauheim, W. Germany.

Also the following kind helpers:

Mrs Ann Baird, Glasgow; Ruth and Eric Bardsley, Bollingon, Cheshire; Gordon Duff, St John's, Newfoundland; A. C. Hughes, Hull; Leonard J. McLaughlin, Montreal; Gilbert E. Porteous, Cardiff; Donald Sanderson, Newcastle upon Tyne; A. A. Smith, Amsterdam; Jeremiah J. Smith, Edinburgh; Theodore Vokos, Piraeus, Greece (Editor 'Naftiliaki'); Mrs D. Wetterhahn, London.

Finally the authors express their thanks to the many newspapers and magazines which helped in the quest for veterans of SC7, and in particular to the following: *Daily Telegraph*; *Flying Angel*; *Hull Daily Mail*; *Montreal Star*; *The Navy*; *Navy News*; *Newcastle Evening Chronicle*; *Scottish Daily Express*; *Sea Breezes*; *Wexford People*; *Manchester Evening News*; *Liverpool Echo*; *Bridport News*.

Index

PQ17 – CONVOY TO HELL

by Paul Lund and Harry Ludlam

In June, 1942, Convoy PQ17, consisting of thirty-five merchant ships, set out for Russia with an escort of cruisers and destroyers. They had a reasonable chance of success until the order came to 'Scatter!'

What followed represents one of the most terrible and tragic blunders of the Second World War.

Authors Ludlam and Lund give a first hand account of the horror and despair that faced the men left to the mercy of a cruel enemy. From thousands of sources and recollections they have built up an unforgettable picture of what it was like to be in PQ17 – and survive . . .

NEW ENGLISH LIBRARY

THE FLEET THAT HAD TO DIE

by Richard Hough

In 1904 the Tsar ordered the Russian fleet to seek out and destroy the Japanese navy. The fleet consisted of about fifty out-dated men-of-war, ill-equipped, badly manned, incompetently officered. They had to sail half-way around the world to engage the armed might of the Japanese navy under the formidable Admiral Togo.

This is the magnificent chronicle of a suicidal venture, doomed to disaster from the start – a voyage that went from catastrophe to catastrophe, ending in bloody and final disaster at the Battle of Tsu-Shima.

NEW ENGLISH LIBRARY

THE HUNTING OF FORCE Z

by Richard Hough

Force Z was the name given to the British battlefleet that sailed to Singapore in the autumn of 1941. Its mission – to defend the whole of both Australia and New Zealand should Japan declare war.

But behind the name hid only the battered *Prince of Wales* and the twenty-five year-old cruiser *Repulse*. And they arrived in the East only five days before Japan attacked Pearl Harbour.

Richard Hough, author of THE FLEET THAT HAD TO DIE and THE POTEMKIN MUTINY, vividly describes the ensuing tragedy and charts in detail the controversial action taken by Force Z's admiral, Tom Phillips.

NEW ENGLISH LIBRARY